Nora started writing in high school and continued through to college while working full time. She worked in the government service in the Philippines and also in Taipei for over six years. In Australia, Nora had a banking career before retrenchment. She is now an active member of Sing Australia, Writing NSW and a volunteer at St Vincent de Paul Society. *The Wings that Soared* is her first book.

The Wings that Soared

a memoir

Nora B. Masesar

First published by Nora B. Masesar in 2020
This edition published in 2020 by Nora B. Masesar

Copyright © Nora B. Masesar 2020
The moral right of the author has been asserted.

All rights reserved. This publication (or any part of it) may not be reproduced or transmitted, copied, stored, distributed or otherwise made available by any person or entity (including Google, Amazon or similar organisations), in any form (electronic, digital, optical, mechanical) or by any means (photocopying, recording, scanning or otherwise) without prior written permission from the publisher.

The Wings that Soared
a memoir

EPUB: 9781922389497
POD: 9781922389503

Cover design by Red Tally Studios

Publishing services provided by Critical Mass
www.critmassconsulting.com

To Davis and Daina

and in loving memory of my parents, brothers and sister.

Contents

Prologue   1
Chapter 1
    Our land and life on the farm   4
Chapter 2
    Tatay's ingenuity   12
Chapter 3
    Our food and water supply   21
Chapter 4
    Our awesome escapades   33
Chapter 5
    Pastimes on the farm   38
Chapter 6
    Locust infestation and life after farming   44
Chapter 7
    My grandfather, unusual stories and phenomenon   46
Chapter 8
    School declaimer, Miss Stamp   52
Chapter 9
    Primary graduation, mementoes   61
Chapter 10
    Sad family event, harvest adventure   64
Chapter 11
    Truth of family breakup and transition to a new life   71
Chapter 12
    Household chores, birth of youngest brother   78

Chapter 13
   High school and post high school years   83
Chapter 14
   Employment as stenographer   89
Chapter 15
   Life as a working student, harsh realities   94
Chapter 16
   Writing experience, Nanay's schooling   101
Chapter 17
   Marriage, early signs of trouble and birth of son   106
Chapter 18
   Work venture in Taipei, dilemma of pregnancy   111
Chapter 19
   Life in Taipei, birth of daughter   118
Chapter 20
   The joys of motherhood   127
Chapter 21
   Office city move, a new live-in nanny   131
Chapter 22
   Marital trouble, chaos at work   134
Chapter 23
   Approval of migration to Australia, left Taipei   139
Chapter 24
   Arrival in Australia and settling in   144
Chapter 25
   Cultural shock experience
   House in Roselands and children's high school friends   149
Chapter 26
   First death in the family, arrival of parents in Australia   158
Chapter 27
   Long drive around Australia, retrenchment   164

Contents

Chapter 28
  Heartaches, blessings, travels to Berlin and historic
  places   168
Chapter 29
  Divorce, new job and overseas workmates   177
Chapter 30
  A joyous birthday occasion, death of brother   182
Chapter 31
  Traumatic effects of divorce, Dad in nursing home,
  meeting Sam   188
Chapter 32
  Canadian holiday   194
Chapter 33
  Davis' graduation, wedding in UK, Europe holiday,
  Davis' job overseas   201
Chapter 34
  Surprise holiday for Nanay and Sam, Davis back home   220
Chapter 35
  Visit to Taipei, first visit to my birthplace   229
Chapter 36
  Second retrenchment, unexpected encounters
  on holidays Two simultaneous deaths   243
Chapter 37
  Island-hopping in the Philippines   251
Chapter 38
  A new course in life and moving forward   257
Chapter 39
  The path I have chosen, our journey in life   261

Glossary   267
Acknowledgements   273

If Winter comes can Spring be far behind? – Ode to the West Wind
Our sweetest songs are those that tell of saddest thought. – To a Skylark

Percy Bysshe Shelley

Prologue

Faith and determination have shaped my destiny. This is a story about a life's journey from childhood to adulthood which shows that dreams, no matter how far-fetched, can be achieved.

The story starts with my childhood spent on the farm in the Philippines. We had a simple life. On the farm we children had awesome and daring escapades. We lived close to nature and learned the basic skills of survival. My primary education was wonderful. It taught me how to become an achiever.

I consider my childhood the happiest years of my life. It was a time of innocent bliss where nature abounded and no rules applied except the discipline of our parents and teachers. I was always with my elder brother and sister who were also my closest friends. Our escapades are worth remembering. We were together as a happy family – until something happened that changed it all. After my primary schooling, our life was hardship, suffering and struggle for survival.

This book also describes how I faced and surmounted obstacles in my life; how I looked at life differently; how I appreciated the beauty of the many blessings I received despite the difficulties – my travels to Asia, America, and Europe, the lessons I learned from the people I met; how we lived our life in Australia; the humour in some experiences; and how God has shaped me to be who I am.

I have accomplished something that I am proud of. Through sheer determination and a strong focus on my goal, I was able to leave my homeland and venture to foreign countries where I knew no one.

I went through a traumatic divorce, deaths in the family, two retrenchments and finally, I have reached a time of freedom to enjoy life. After my divorce, I couldn't look back without tears in my eyes. I remembered all the sorrows. My grief made me emotionally fragile. It hurt me deeply despite my determination to move on. I chose to switch off certain parts of my life, to blot out the hurt that had not abated despite the long years of trying to move forward. As the years went by and as I became older, I gained a mature acceptance of what happened. I began to set aside my emotional baggage and really started living. I discovered that happiness is not at the end of the journey, but it is the journey itself.

I could have done things differently. But it was my life, my journey and I did it my own way. I have no regrets. In this memoir, I express my feelings as I discuss each passage of my life. The aim is not to please everyone.

I abided by the strict rules and guidance of my parents. I was obedient, I followed the rules, but that is over now. I am proud of what I have accomplished and of what I have become. I must have inherited my mother's resilience and wisdom and my father's courage and determination. The legacy of my parents' wisdom, especially my mother's, has been handed down to my children. I hope it will be handed down to the next and future generations.

My brothers and sister – Kuya Tito, Ate Vernie, Frank and Benjamin – are gone from this life. They were brave because they knew they were dying, but they faced the eventuality of death. My father and my mother have also passed away, but their legacy of love, strength and determination lives on. As devastated as I was at the loss of loved ones, I knew life had to move on. And so must I.

Chapter 1

I was born in Madong, a small barrio in Janiuay, Iloilo, Philippines. Iloilo is one of the islands in the middle part of the Philippines called the Visayas. We lived on the farm my father tilled. Seven of us brothers and sisters were born on the farm, delivered by a midwife. Only my younger brother Frank was born in the hospital. I was the third child in the family.

My father was a jack of all trades. He was not only a farmer but also a carpenter and a merchant. He was ingenious and resourceful. His innovations made the work practices of most of his co-farmers in the surrounding barrio pale in comparison. My father's ingenuity brought much meaning into our lives.

The happiest days of my life were spent on the farm. I was always close to my elder brother and sister. It was a time of pure bliss and innocence. We were free to roam the fields, climb trees, explore the rice fields, go to the creek where we swam and caught fish, play hide and seek and devise our own games to entertain ourselves. We had no fear of exploring our surroundings because we felt safe in our neighbourhood.

Madong was a small barrio where everyone knew one another even if they were kilometres away. We enjoyed just being children and had a life full of fun. We were close to nature, the trees, animals and insects. We were free to play and do our own thing, so long as we pay heed when Nanay, our mother, called us for lunch or dinner – otherwise we'd be in big trouble.

The Masesar land in Madong was 2.3 hectares. It was sold to the Maranon family and the proceeds of the land were divided between the Masesar brothers and sisters. Uncle Hugo, the eldest in the family, took his share of the proceeds and went with his family to Mindanao Island in the south of the Philippines. There he established a trucking and logging business. A few years later, he sold the business and took his entire family to Canada. The remaining brothers and sisters stayed in the Philippines. My father, Tatay, took his share of the proceeds from the land sale and remained in Madong. He leased the land sold to the Maranons and also tilled adjacent lands in Tuburan, leased from a Chinese man called Apoy Wong. Tatay tilled these farmlands mainly as rice fields divided by rice paddies. He employed people to help plant and harvest the rice.

We elder children helped with the farm work. Kuya Tito, Ate Vernie and I were not exempted from the hard work as Tatay always needed a helping hand to work on the land he tilled as well as looking after the fields of vegetables and fruits for our needs. We also helped with the poultry, in the piggery, and in all aspects of farm work to sustain our livelihood. Nanay's older nieces and nephews helped her look after us children while she devoted her time to managing the day-to-day activities of domestic work – cooking, cleaning, laundry and helping my father in the management of the farm.

Tatay was ingenious. Whatever he did had to be perfect, including farming. Tatay applied the Masagana system of planting rice. It was a 12 by 12 planting layout, so from whichever angle you looked at it – vertically, diagonally or horizontally – you could see a straight line between the rice seedlings. This method proved to be the best system for rice farming. Our rice production at the end of the harvest was always plentiful.

The rice seedlings we planted came from the seedbeds that Tatay planted before the start of the planting season. When the seedbeds were ready for planting, he hired workers from neighbouring barrios to plant the rice from morning till dusk. It was a joy to look at the rice fields, neat in their patterns, when the planting season was finished. The Masagana system allowed the rice to grow tall and abundant. If there were weeds, they were easy to spot, giving Tatay time to eradicate them before they grew into the planted rice.

The Filipino folk song 'Planting Rice is Never Fun' describes this hard work well.

> Planting rice is never fun
> Bent from morn till the set of sun
> Cannot stand and cannot sit
> Cannot rest for a little bit.

The Tagalog version has a second verse which goes like this:

> Sa umaga pagkagising
> Ay agad iisipin
> Kung saan may patanim
> Duon may masarap na pagkain.

Roughly translated, this means as soon as you wake up in the morning think straight ahead to rice planting. It is where you will find delicious food.

Some say planting rice is discouraging because it is never fun. Actually, this is true. As the daughter of a rice farmer I know that planting rice is hard work, a back-breaking job, but a job that has to be done. You cannot stand and cannot sit; you just bend to plant rice in the soft muddy soil. The only chance to stand up is to collect more bundled rice seedlings from the rice beds or take a lunch break.

Nanay would rouse us at around 4 am to go to the rice fields. She'd survey the fields and point to the area where we had to start planting rice as the day broke. Sometimes we were out planting rice before the sun rose as it's too hot when the sun is up. If Tatay hired labourers, then we children were expected to go with the hired hands to plant rice with them. Tatay had the rice seedlings ready and bundled before the day of planting. The hired planters did not need to pull them from the seedbed when they arrived.

We ploughed the fields in rows before the planting day. This guided the rice planters as to where to plant the seedlings in a uniform manner. They could easily push the seedlings deep into the soil in a straight line. Our working carabaos (water buffaloes) were harnessed to pull the ploughs. Usually, twenty or more workers came during the day, the men taking turns to plough the fields. This enabled us to finish planting rice quicker and cover several paddies. Rice planting was done during the rainy months. The monsoon rains usually start in June and continue until August.

I was young and little, but I ventured into the rice field holding a plough. The only problem was the water buffalo got impatient with me because I was so awkward handling the reins. We always ended up in disaster. I often lost control and plunged into the mud while holding onto the rope pulled along by the water buffalo – without the plough. For anybody watching, it would have been hilarious. Ploughing rice fields was a great experience for me but also exasperating. I had to try several times to get it right but even at a young age, I did not give up easily. I was lucky if I ploughed a whole row without mishap. This, for me, was a great accomplishment – something to brag about to the family.

The worst part of planting rice was touching the worms attached to the seedlings and the leeches that clung to my legs and arms and sucked my blood. The leeches were slimy and difficult to remove as they clung hard. They would fall if a pinch of salt was rubbed on them, but we did not have that luxury in the field. It was usually my elder sister who came to my rescue to remove these parasites when I screamed my head off in panic and disgust. But this was part of farm life. Despite my revulsion, I had to keep going and finish the work. We had to finish our assigned tasks. With this responsibility in mind, I accepted the hazards despite my fear.

The best part of all this hard work was when we rested and ate lunch or took our mid-afternoon snacks. Nanay's role was to feed us. Lunch consisted mostly of rice, fish and vegetables. Tatay or Nanay would go to the markets to buy fish and other provisions for us and the workers who helped us plant the rice. This was in addition to the fish we caught from the river and the freshly harvested vegetables from our gardens.

Alternatively, a pig would be slaughtered to supply our meat during the planting season. We had chickens from our poultry shed and ducks from the ponds if Tatay had no time to slaughter a pig. For our merienda (teatime), we had guinatan halo-halo, a mixture of sweet potatoes, ripe native banana, purple taro called ube, tapioca and ripe shredded jackfruit flesh to give the guinatan a beautiful flavour and aroma. If tapioca wasn't available, we made small balls called bilo-bilo out of glutinous rice. This delicacy was cooked in coconut milk and brown sugar. When the guinatan was nearly cooked, the coconut cream was added to thicken the consistency. It was yummy and very filling – one of my favourite snacks.

We occasionally had puto, made of ground glutinous rice. We poured it into a round tin with a banana leaf at the base and cooked it over burning coals. When the puto was cooked, it was topped with freshly grated coconut. If Tatay had time to go to town to buy groceries, we had margarine to spread over it. It just melted on top of the delicacy when hot, making the puto a mouth-watering snack. Another variety of snack from this ground glutinous rice is palitaw. Literally, it means floating. This is a flattened oblong lump of ground glutinous rice dropped into boiling water. When it floats on top of the water, it is cooked and ready to be taken out. We dip this palitaw in sugar with sesame seeds. For added flavour, we sprinkle it with freshly grated coconut. We also had bibingka made out of whole glutinous rice cooked in a clay pot. Nanay mixed it with coconut cream and brown sugar and cooked it in a big wok (we had no ovens then). When it was cooked, Nanay would flatten the bibingka on a wide circular shallow basket covered at the base with banana leaves. Then she made crispy coconut bits to sprinkle on top. These home-made delicacies were cooked freshly each day to give a variety of snacks for the hard-working people planting rice in our fields.

Tatay was the sole supervisor of our rice growing. If there were weeds between the rows of the planted rice, we helped him pull them out. Eventually, due to the large area of land that Tatay tilled, he used chemicals to eradicate the vicious weeds without affecting the growing rice. At harvest time, Tatay hired the same people who helped us plant the rice. Some of them were from neighbouring barrios.

When we harvested rice, the male workers used a big scythe to cut the rice stalks before bundling them. The women and girls used a small scythe wedged on a bamboo stick tied to our right hand – just the size to fit into our hands. We women were slower to harvest rice this way because we cut the stalks near the rice grains and it was harder to bind them into bundles. The stalks were shorter, but our harvested rice was tidier than the men's bundled ones with long stalks that included weeds with them. We used a salakot (a triangular hat made of bamboo slats) to protect us from the heat of the sun. We bound this hat with a bandana tied around our necks so it would not fly when the wind blew.

Before sundown, we all carried our bundled rice to the place where Tatay had spread several mats made from nipa leaves. We placed the bundles of rice on these laid-out mats and stayed with our bundles until the harvested rice was accounted for. Hired labourers got bundles of rice as payment, depending on how much they had harvested. One variety of rice we grew was tall. The wind swept them in one direction when the rice was heavy with grain. They stayed in that direction until they were ready to be harvested.

If I remember right, the ratio of sharing the harvest was 3:1. One bundle went to the landlord, one bundle to us who managed the farm, and one bundle to the worker. Our share was the same ratio as the workers. I don't know whether Tatay got an additional share from the landlords. They were well-off. One was a wealthy Chinese businessman in town. The counting of and accounting for the harvested rice was done daily. The share due to the landlord was placed in our rice granary. When the granary was filled, the landlord would come to take his share of the harvest.

We processed our share of the harvest manually. We used our feet (linas) on a big mat or in a tub to remove the grains of rice from the stalks. When we finished, we spread the rice grains on big mats to dry under the sun. When the grains were dry, we removed pulp from the rice with a pestle and mortar. Afterwards, we used a flat round basket to sieve the skin from the clean rice. Because it was hard work and it took time to do this, we processed just enough for our immediate use. Tatay went to town to process the remaining rice. This was how we had sacks of rice stored in our rice granary and used for our staple food supply until the next harvest season.

Chapter 2

My father, Leon Masesar, was given the award of First Farmer of the Year in the 1950s. The Bureau of Plant Industry, now part of Department of Natural Resources, gave the award to my father for producing 240 cavans of rice per hectare, making him the highest rice production farmer in Iloilo province. A cavan was a Spanish unit for measuring rice in the Philippines. There is no exact equivalent in current measurements but a near approximation would be around 50–56 kilos per cavan.

Between the rice seasons my father, with the family's help, planted maize or corn, sweet potatoes, cassavas, peanuts, pumpkins, other root crops and vegetables, and fruit for our consumption to sustain us during the year. Tatay bought additional rice from town if our harvest during the rice season was insufficient. This might be due to unforeseen events like locust infestation or flooding that destroyed our rice production.

Tatay carved our mortar and pestle from a big tree trunk. The mortar resembled a small boat (approximately 140" x 40") with a big smooth round hole in the middle. The long pestle had a grip in the middle with round ends on both sides so that either side could be used. We normally had two pestles. When there was a lot of rice to pound, two people used the pestle alternately to finish the job quickly. The same thing applied when we wanted to make delicacies that required mixing ingredients. Both flat ends of the mortar were a convenient place for us to put plates, cups and ingredients like additional soft green rice (pinipig), bananas, grated coconuts and red sugar for the delicacy we were making.

Tatay also made a big round stone grinder to grind our corn and rice. One heavy round stone was placed on top of the other stone with a space between them. There was a hole in the middle where we poured the grains of rice or maize. We rotated the pulley handle attached to the top of the upper stone to grind the rice or maize that had been wedged between these two stones. The finer grains flowed into the concave tunnel carved on the lower stone. Then it fell onto the round flat basket on the floor which caught the grains.

Whether we used the pestle and mortar to remove the pulp of rice grains or use the grinder stone to grind, the process of making the rice grains ready for cooking was hard work. On the other hand, it was fascinating to learn this crude, manual way of doing things. (I found that mixing the ground grain of corn with the newly harvested rice actually tasted good.)

As jack of all trades, Tatay was also our medicine man. Whenever we had a wound, he would scrape something from a yellowish stone which he said had a curative effect. Indeed, it did, as the wound healed quickly when this powdery substance was administered. I know now that the yellow stone was sulphur.

One time Kuya Tito, Ate Vernie and I were running around, playing in our earthen yard. I stepped on a rusty nail and it was imbedded in my left foot. I must have screamed loudly because Tatay and Nanay were with us immediately. I was lucky they were home and not working on the fields. Tatay cut an incision on my foot, squeezed out a lot of blood, poured alcohol and Mercurochrome (equivalent to iodine) and after drying the wound, scraped a lot of match heads on the wound and lighted it. The only thing I remembered was circumnavigating the entire balcony area on my bottom while holding onto my foot. I can't remember what else was done to it, but my wound healed quickly. I walked around with a bandaged foot for a week and that was it! The bandage we used was a strip of calico or white cloth tied around the wounded area to protect it from infection and dirt. We didn't have disposable bandages. After that, I never walked barefoot. That must be why at a young age, I was the only one in the farm who wore wooden sandals every day, and the only one who wore them at school. Most of my classmates went barefoot.

Tatay had a healing hand. He knew the pressure points to massage when we weren't feeling well. News of his healing gift spread in the barrio. Some of our neighbours asked for his ministrations if they wanted to get well. Tatay used a sweet-smelling oil after the massage, either coconut oil we made ourselves or Efficascent oil that he bought in town.

Living on the farm meant living close to nature so a lot of unusual things happened in our daily life. I remember the day my younger brother Ben was placed inside a big wooden basket which served as a playpen. We were working in the fields planting vegetable seedlings in the newly ploughed rows. Tatay was always particular about how to plant crops so as to produce the best harvest. We were farther down the field when we heard a loud scream from the basket. We all ran back to see what had happened. Nanay pulled my brother out from the basket. She was nearby minding him but she was also busy planting seeds like us. All we saw when we came to the rescue were a lot of red ants that had bitten my brother, crawling inside the basket. No wonder he screamed loud and shrill.

On the farm you could see lizards crawling, some of them with beautiful colours. The largest ones were called tuko because they made this onomatopoeic *tu-ko* sound at night-time. You couldn't see where they were hiding but could hear them. Sometimes they crawled out from their hiding place, and we saw how big they were. They weren't dangerous, so we lived in peace with them. Nanay told us of one instance when she saw a green snake curled up on top of our mosquito net when she woke up one morning. She only shooed it away as we didn't kill these creatures. They were part of our farm existence. The rats and mosquitoes were different because they were pests. Rats ate our rice. The mosquito bites were itchy and dreadful, so they needed to be eradicated. I was not aware of malaria during our time.

Life on the farm had taught us how to survive and become resilient by learning basic skills. I learned to cut wood using an axe; learned how to build a fire without a match using the sun's rays; fetched water with a pail from the well, and later on filled hollow long bamboo poles with water. I could never balance a water jar on my head so that was out of the question. I was too unstable and not still enough for such a task.

I learned to dig cassava roots, sweet potatoes and other root crops. It gave me the creeps though, when I happened to dig the big worms underneath the soil. When we worked on our vegetable garden, we used spade, rake, hoe and pick. We didn't have garden gloves. We fetched water from the well that Father dug for us to water our plants and crops. It was hard work, but we couldn't wait until the rain watered them. We had tropical weather so when it rained, it poured. We looked forward to it as it was the best time for us children to clean ourselves. We splashed water around and enjoyed the strong downspouts on our heads from the roof gutter. It was fun! It also meant that we didn't have to fetch water from the well.

Tatay had a catchment that channelled the water to the big drum he propped up on a platform with wooden walls to secure it. It had a small tap at the bottom, so we needn't go up the ladder to get water. After the rain, the best pastime for us children were to fish in the stream down the road. It was a joy to catch fish and sometimes shrimps that wriggled in our nets until Nanay cooked them. If there was flood after a storm, we explored the following day. The rice fields overflowed with water and looked like a lake. We were careful to only walk on the roads because the rice fields were deep and there was no sense getting stuck in the mud in the middle of nowhere with no help at hand.

Our house was a traditional nipa hut, made of nipa leaves and bamboo poles. This was typical in the Philippines and part of Filipino culture.

Tatay built our house large enough to accommodate us seven children plus the live-in helpers, one handyman and two of my elder female cousins on Nanay's side. The entrance to the house on the ground floor led to an earthen lounge where there were long bamboo benches made by Tatay. Midway was a ladder to the upper floor with an open wide lounge room. On both sides were rooms divided by thatched walls.

The main bedroom on the right belonged to my parents. We children slept together in the spacious lounge room. The door leading to the left led to a long wide space and a balcony overlooking the rice fields. The flooring on this upper level was made of bamboo slats and the walls were thatched with bamboo frames. The windows opened outwards. During our time, our furniture was basic – wooden or bamboo chests, chairs, long benches, a rocking chair and wooden beds.

Most of the household things were kept on the ground floor. Our rice and corn stone grinder were there. Near the back of the house was the granary where Tatay kept our rice supply. Tatay's farming and carpentry materials were also on this floor. The flooring on this area was just the natural earth. Our pestle and mortar carved from a big piece of wood was near the kitchen. Further down the hall, we had an elevated kitchen built of bamboo slat flooring and thatched walls. The windows here also opened outwards. We used clay pots for cooking rice and fish, and steel pots for vegetables. We had a wok for frying. We placed banana leaves at the bottom of the pots to prevent the food from burning. The pots either sat on holes held by four crossed steel bars on top of the fire or on a cement stove with holes on top of a burning fire. We lit piled sticks and chopped wood at the bottom of the pots to make a fire. The charcoal produced from these pieces of wood and sticks was gathered to fill the iron if there was ironing to be done during the day. On either side of the ladder going to the kitchen was a door. The right door led to the side of the house where we could go under the house and out to the flower garden. This was also a way of going out onto the earthen road Tatay built for our use. The left door opened towards fruit trees. On this side were the duck pond and the pigpen. The chickens were on another side of the house protected by wire mesh.

Fresh vegetables came from our gardens. We had all types of vegetables. The song 'Bahay Kubo' includes the kinds of vegetables and crops that surround a farmhouse. Some of the varieties of vegetables can only be found in Asia. We also had different varieties of bananas – my favourite was called saba, a squarish variety. When it's ripe, you can eat it raw, boiled or mixed with other ingredients to make guinatan halo-halo.

Around the house were trees that provided us with ample fruit. Different trees bore fruit at different times. We had several varieties planted a few metres away from the house to cater for each season. There was an abundance of papaya (paw paw) trees with fruit that grew in clusters. We used the green ones as a vegetable in chicken stew, seasoned with ginger and chilli leaves. When they were ripe, they were eaten as a normal fruit. Sometimes we added condensed milk to make an afternoon snack or a dessert.

Tatay had a separate elevated field for our fruit and vegetable crops. We loved helping Tatay plant the vegetables and root crops. There were lots of pumpkins, sunflowers, sweet potatoes and all sorts of fresh vegetables and root crops in the field including ginger, garlic, shallots, tomatoes, eggplants, snake beans, peas, bitter gourd, sesame plants, carrots, peanuts and cassavas. Our vegetable field was near the water well that Tatay dug. This was where we fetched drinking water, where we took showers, laundered clothes and watered the crops. Tatay made a dirt road for us from the well to the house. He demonstrated ingenuity in all these things.

We were young, so it was hard for us to fetch water from the well, carrying a pail in each hand. Most of the time we spilled half the contents before we reached the house. To enable us to fetch water from the well without mishap, Tatay made us big long bamboo poles. He removed and cleaned the inside mid-section of a big bamboo pole to enable the water to go through to the bottom, leaving the end intact to hold water. It was easier for us children to fetch water this way because we could put it on our shoulders, switching from one to the other.

Our corn had a field separate from the other crops. We delighted in dropping corn or maize seeds on ploughed areas of the field during the dry season. Sometimes Tatay got seeds of different varieties of corn. As well as yellow corn, we had mixed white and yellow corn, which was soft to bite and had a glutinous, sticky consistency when cooked. When it was ripe, we loved picking the ears of the corn. Mostly, we boiled them for a nourishing snack. I loved the yellow hair of the corn, so I gathered them to make a pretty doll with yellow hair. I made my doll out of gingham cloth stuffed with kapok, a cotton-like substance. I drew the eyes, eyebrows, nose and lips with coloured pencils before sewing coloured thread over my drawings.

Our papayas bore fruits in clusters. The green ones we cooked with chicken and Moringa leaves we call malunggay, a plant with leaves shaped like a four-leaf clover. This vegetable grew in abundance. We usually washed it and ran our fingers through the stem to scrape the leaves. We needed a container full of these leaves to have enough leaves to cook with chicken, green papaya and fresh ginger. We called this dish tinola and the soup was a very effective treatment for a cold. When the papayas ripened, we ate them as a refreshing snack. Our papaya varieties are very sweet when ripe.

The banana trees planted on the rice paddies were big and numerous and produced better fruits than those on the higher land. We had different varieties of bananas.

There were pomelo trees in front of the house and a star apple tree called kaymito. Kaymito fruit when ripe is a green round fruit with soft white flesh. There is also a purple variety. We scooped the soft flesh with a spoon, or just broke the skin and sucked the white flesh. The star apple tree has a sticky white juice that is hard to remove because it sticks like glue. When we had a stomach upset, we boiled the leaves of this tree and drank the juice to stop diarrhoea. It worked like a Kaopectate medicine.

There were chicos (Sapodilla, a brown round sweet fruit) and different varieties of guavas near the road to our house. The fruits of the native ones were small and hard, but the imported varieties, especially the Indonesian one, had large, sweet fruit. We had seneguelas (a small round fruit which was a greenish-purple colour when ripe), camachiles (a tamarind-shaped fruit with a bland taste and colour ranging from green or yellow to purple when ripe) and balimbing, a fruit which tastes sweet-sour and looks like a star when cut horizontally.

We also had jackfruit trees which yielded a lot of fruit. We cooked the green, raw ones as a vegetable. It tasted nice with a slice of pork or shrimp, with coconut cream and chilli to season. When the jackfruits were ripe, they emitted a beautiful aromatic smell. We removed the flesh from the spiky skin to eat or used it to flavour teatime delicacies like guinatan. We also sprinkled shredded pieces of ripe jackfruit over bibingka. The seeds were boiled and eaten as nuts. They were soft and fleshy, like chestnuts. We had avocadoes and guayabanos too. Guayabano fruit looked like custard apples. It had spiky skin and a sweet-sour taste when ripe.

Our coconut buko trees were on the opposite side of the road from our house, bearing large clusters of coconuts. We had a kapok tree that we used as stuffing in our pillows. It was fun harvesting the fluffy white cotton from the kapok tree, although it made us sneeze.

Chapter 3

Our food mainly consisted of rice, vegetables and fish. We had corn, cassava, squash (pumpkin) and kamote (sweet potatoes) growing in the fields for food supplements.

The fish from the markets were always fresh. My favourites were galunggong, sapsap, tilapia, anchovies, sardines, bilong-bilong and shrimps. Nanay could make delicious fish dishes just using salt, tomatoes, ginger and seneguelas or gabi (taro) leaves. Sometimes she fried the fish with a sprinkle of salt. She cooked shrimps with saluyot (a native green leafy vegetable) and freshly grated bamboo shoots. This tasted good with coconut milk or cream and small red chillies. The red and green chillies were grown in our backyard. We cooked milk fish (bangus) in different ways. Nanay prepared fish simply – she either cooked it with green leafy vegetables, onions and tomatoes, making a soup, or grilled it in charcoal wrapped with banana leaves and seasoned with finely chopped tomatoes, onions and ginger stuffed in the slit stomach of the fish.

When Nanay needed vegetables, my elder sister Ate Vernie was always in charge of getting them. She would take her long hacking knife and go out to the fields without hesitation. I used to tag along to see how and where she found them. She could topple a banana trunk with the big hacking knife. First, she chopped off the bunch of fruits, then she opened the trunk of the banana tree to get the soft core inside. The core was cooked with green leafy vegetables, meat or shrimp. Nanay sometimes added coconut cream and small red chillies to give it extra flavour.

If we wanted fresh mushrooms, we had to wake up early in the morning to get the best and biggest. These grew on molehills and also on the plains, sprouting from dried rice or cogon grass. At our young age, we knew how to recognise the edible mushrooms from the poisonous ones. If we woke late, we only found the smaller mushrooms just sprouting from the molehills. The neighbours had already picked up the nice big ones. We were lucky if they missed the medium sized ones.

Our food flavouring was shrimp paste that my parents bought from the markets. It was called ginamos, a delicacy in Visayan province. It made any vegetable dish taste good. We also had fish sauce called patis which was nice when we sautéd different types of vegetables like pumpkin, bitter gourd, eggplants, okra and a few small shrimps to go with it. On its own, shrimp paste was nice to eat with a few small red chillies as an appetiser and condiment to the native dishes. One of our tongue-watering indulgences was to dip the sliced green or almost ripe, crispy mango into the fish sauce with chilli. We could always concoct something pleasant to the palate.

During the rainy season, we children roamed the fields after the floods and would find fresh fish floating or wriggling on the clear running water on the roads. They were flat white fish with scales like silver biddies. We also found pantat or hito (which looked like eels) in the rice fields, kuhol (escargot), clinging to harvested rice stalks, crabs from the sandy part of the field and fresh shrimps from the stream. The fresh shrimps and fresh fish floating on the clear running water on the roads after the flood may have come from the creek nearby when it overflowed.

On the farm, we learned to eat different kinds of fish, even those with plenty of bones. We knew how to eat them with rice and vegetables without getting pricked by the bones. If, on occasion, we accidentally had a little bone stuck in our throat, Nanay would give us a piece of banana to swallow. Most of the time, we continued eating as if nothing happened. I can't remember ever going to the doctor because of fish bones. Another food we learned how to suck properly out of its shell were the spiral snails called suso. We sucked it with an inward whooping smack of our lips like a loud kiss, and out came the contents. At other times we took it out from the shell with a toothpick. This was cooked like an escargot. I liked it when Nanay cooked it with ginger and coconut cream with a bit of fresh red chilli.

Our rice always tasted good because we processed it ourselves. We put tanglad (lemon grass) in the pot when cooking to give it a beautiful aroma. Sometimes we had a special breakfast of champorado made out of glutinous rice mixed with dark cocoa and brown sugar. We ate this with salted dried herring called tuyo. Although it stinks when cooked, it has a salty nice flavour when eaten with champorado. This dried fish was a native favourite that went well with freshly cooked rice and sliced tomatoes. We had our own cocoa plants and I had seen brown cacao fruits, but I didn't know how it looked after it was processed. Nanay bought pure dark cocoa from the market and showed us the round sliced dark brown cocoa before she cooked it. It was in the shape of a big round tablet wrapped in brown paper. Nanay would also make a breakfast drink out of these dark cocoa chocolate tablets. It made a rich, dark beautiful drink. We added brown sugar and cow or goat's milk if available.

We had fresh buko juice from young green coconuts. There was nothing wasted from the coconut – we scraped the soft tender flesh of the coconut out of the shell after we finished the juice. If we wanted variety, we split open the coconut shell, scraped the soft tender flesh, scooped it out and placed it in a tall glass, adding sugar and milk. It is also nice to eat it as it is. In those days, restaurants served coconut juice, opening the top of the fresh coconut to insert a straw. If it was served in a glass, they scraped the soft flesh from inside the fruit so the customers could drink the juice and spoon the flesh from the glass.

We made several kinds of snacks out of bananas as well as eating them as a healthy fruit. Saba bananas could be eaten fresh when ripe or cooked. We could boil it or fry it wrapped in thin pastry with ripe jackfruit sprinkled with brown sugar. We could mix it with other ingredients to make halo-halo, or cook it in a dish called pochero, a pork stew mixed with cooking bananas and bok choy leaves.

There were a lot of sources for our vegetable supply. We found young bamboo shoots sprouting at the base of the tall bamboo trees that grew near the stream. We'd crawl under the bamboos to get them. After we sliced the bamboo shoots thinly, Nanay cooked them with coconut cream, shrimp, a bit of chilli and leafy green vegetables. We also ate sweet potato leaves and pumpkin flowers. Sweet potato leaves blend well with boiled mung beans or stewed fish. The pumpkin flowers went well with other vegetables sautéed with a little bit of pork, chicken or shrimp. When we picked the leaves of the pumpkin and sweet potatoes, we left the vines intact so the crops would grow naturally, producing their root crops.

We had eggplants, shallots, tomatoes, okra, snake beans, peas – all kinds of vegetables. Tatay's pumpkins were the greenish ones. They grew so big that even with a big family like ours, one whole pumpkin was more than enough. We left half for another day's cooking. Corn, sweet potatoes and cassavas were boiled mostly for morning and afternoon snacks.

We planted sunflowers on the side of the mud road that Tatay made. I learnt something from Tatay about the sunflower. He said that the sunflower's head followed the movements of the sun. This was where it got the name sunflower. As a curious child, I was fascinated to find out whether Tatay was right. I watched it the whole day. When the sun rose from the east, the flowers faced that way; at noontime, the heads were up. At sundown, the sunflower faced towards the west. It was true! My father was a good mentor. When the sunflower finished its term, the roots were extracted and replaced by another root crop, usually cassava. We then extracted the seeds from the sunflower, dried and spread them evenly on a wide mat to dry in the sun. When thoroughly dried, they were crispy, ready to be eaten as nuts. We also roasted cashew nuts when we sat down together at night in front of a bonfire during our family get-together. Cashews were my favourite nuts because they emit a sweet-smelling aroma when cooked.

Tatay had rows of peanuts in the garden. When they were ready to be harvested, we pulled them out from the soil and let them dry under the sun. We boiled peanuts for snacks or ate them raw when freshly harvested. If we wanted roasted peanuts, we cooked them in a pan. If we wanted to sprinkle the peanuts on the delicacies we were making for teatime, we pounded them in the pestle and mortar. This gave the merienda (teatime) a bit of a nutty flavour.

Cassavas grew under the rich soil in abundance. We used to boil them to make a lot of different snacks. We dipped them into the raw brown sugar or sometimes we pounded them until they became sticky, then added the freshly grated coconut and milk.

We have a delicacy called pinipig, a sweet-smelling soft green rice. We mixed it with sugar, freshly grated coconut, and a bit of milk. We made it into a ground ball when it became sticky like dough. We also added it to halo-halo, the iced drink. This soft green variety was a special kind of rice that few farmers grew for its delicateness. Like glutinous rice, it was grown on the mountainside where the climate was cooler.

Eggs came from our poultry. We loved watching the hens spurt out eggs early in the morning when we came with our baskets to fill for breakfast. Our meat came from the chickens and pigs we raised. We had several water buffaloes, but they were not eaten as they were working animals in the field. They were also used to pull a cart to carry heavy things. Occasionally, we had a goat to slaughter. Goats were not abundant. They were kept mostly to provide milk.

We loved feeding the chicken and the ducks. We were attached to them, and it made us cry if one of our favourites became a treat for lunch or dinner. The ducks sometimes bit my hands when I fed them. They chased us but it was part of the fun. I loved watching them wade in the water going *quack, quack*. They produced larger and firmer eggs than the chickens.

We learned how to dry beef (tapa) from a slaughtered cow and pork from slaughtered pigs. Tapa was a delicacy, crispy and tasty. Nanay fried it and we ate it with rice, tomatoes and shallots. We also loved the anchovies, sapsap and other seafood that Tatay and Nanay bought from the markets. The abundance of our provisions was limitless.

Under Nanay's patient teaching and supervision I learned to build a fire in the earthen stove. I piled dry sticks in a certain way so they held together under the cooking pot. I placed dried cogon leaves or a crumpled newspaper under the sticks, and then started the fire by lighting the flammable ones first. When the wood started burning, I adjusted the amount of flame needed to cook the food on the pot or pans.

We cooked rice in a clay pot with banana leaves at the bottom to prevent it from sticking and burning. Rice tastes better than when it's cooked in a steel pot. We cooked our fish the same way unless we wanted to fry it or wrap it in banana leaves and cook it on charcoal. To roast root crops, we placed them on the charcoal that was still burning after cooking our main dish. In the morning, Nanay would boil ginger ale for a hot beverage. Very rarely, we drank hot chocolate at breakfast. We weren't allowed to drink coffee in my time; only the elders were allowed.

When we had a bruise, Nanay would pick an arapunaya leaf (a purplish coloured leaf with green streaks which probably belongs to the aloe vera family) or a green leaf (what we now call aloe vera) and squeeze the juice over the affected area and bingo! In a few days' time, the bruises or scratches had healed.

During the planting season, I had skin problems due to the prolonged soaking in the mud, wounds from leeches' bites and other skin irritations made worse by my constant scratching. To prevent scars, Nanay would massage my legs with coconut oil. Our coconut oil was always fresh and undiluted. It was very soothing and Nanay had an ample supply. When my skin healed, there were no scars. Nanay also used coconut oil on our whole body after a bath to make our skin smooth.

We had no refrigerator on the farm. We preserved our meats and fish by salting and drying them in the sun covered by protective nets so flies wouldn't contaminate the food. We collected them when thoroughly dried. These dried meats and fish were delicious when cooked because they were crispy and nice to eat with rice, tomatoes and vegetables. Nanay added dried meat to the vegetables she cooked to give extra flavour.

Our meals consisted mainly of rice, fish and fresh vegetables from the gardens. On occasion, we had meat when Nanay cooked chicken or Tatay cooked duck from our pond. He was the only one who could cook duck properly. At other times, Tatay slaughtered a pig, especially when we had visitors or during planting season.

We had several coconut trees that Tatay planted on the side of the road near an old, disused well. The coconuts we harvested were sufficient for our needs. Nothing was wasted. We made buko from the young, green coconut, scraping the soft white meat for a nutritious snack. The core or ubod taken from the top of the coconut palm was used as a salad. It is sold as a delicacy in pastry shops nowadays. Coconut flesh was also used for commercial purposes to make lard, oil, soap and more.

If we wanted to make coconut cream, we scraped the hard, white flesh of the mature coconut with our home-made scraper. The scraper was made of small clustered folded tins with holes on both sides, secured by a long wooden plank. We sat on the wooden plank and scraped the coconut flesh. When all the flesh had been scraped, we placed it on a thin sieving cloth, soaked in a small amount of water, and squeezed the juice out of it. It spurted out a pure, white thickened cream ready to be added to a dish. The coconut cream tasted good when added to a shrimp or chicken dish with vegetables and fresh red chilli.

When Nanay wanted to make oil, she cooked the scraped coconut flesh in a big wok until the oil was extracted. The oil was placed in bottles ready to be used. When freshly made, we used it as body oil. It smelt so good. The crispy brown bits floating on top of the oil were used to sprinkle as topping on a sticky glutinous rice cake called suman, cassava cake or maize pudding. After a few days, we used it for cooking oil.

Tatay made ladles and kitchen utensils, cups and piggybanks out of the dark brown coconut shell, as well as scoops screwed onto a long handle for our drinking water. Before we had taps, we scooped our drinking water from a big clay container called a banga. It was a good way of getting drinking water from the big jar.

We used coconut husks when our bamboo slat flooring was later on changed into wooden floors. We cleaned and polished the floors with floor wax. When the wax was dry, we used our feet to slide coconut husks on the waxed wooden floor. The husks served as hair-like brushes that we moved with our feet back and forth on the waxed wooden floor, making it shiny, gleaming and spotless. We cut the mature coconuts horizontally to make the coconut husks, which we dried in the sun. The brown shell and skin were left intact.

Coconut shells were also used commercially as painted ornaments. In one of our native dances, coconut shell halves were used to produce a cacophony of sounds. In this dance, men attached several coconut shells to their bodies to make harmonious sounds by clicking them when they performed twists and turns while dancing.

The coconut gave us so many benefits that it's hard to believe they came from just one fruit. Amazing! It was like manna from heaven.

Aside from being an edible root crop, cassava had other uses. We made starch from cassava, soaking clothes after the final rinse so that the cotton and linens looked crisp and smooth when ironed.

I learned to make starch from cassava by slicing it thinly, adding a little water, placing the slices in a cream-coloured sack or calico cloth, tying it with a string, and squeezing the juice out of it. I then added hot water to make it sticky, stirring it to the desired consistency. When the starch was made, I added just enough water to retain the sticky consistency and immediately submerged our cotton clothes in it, especially school uniforms, blouses, pants and balloon skirts. After drying on the clothesline, we ironed them. Our iron was made of heavy steel with an opening at the back of the base and a latch to close it after we filled it with burning charcoal. If we needed to iron more clothes, we had to make sure we had enough burning logs to replace the ones that died down.

Our first source of water was the well that Tatay dug a few metres from the house. He built an earthen pathway to the well so it would be easy for us to go there and fill our pail of water or the long bamboo pole. It was hard to carry water with a pail because it spilled while we walked. It was almost half-empty before we even reached the house. The big bamboo pole was a lot safer and carried more water. We learned how to balance the bamboo pole on our shoulders. We filled big water containers from the well. We also had a big banga for our drinking water. Tatay placed a strainer below the lid and attached a tap to the bottom of the banga so we could have clean, cool, crisp drinking water.

When the neighbours learned about the well, they took water for free and without permission. They also laundered their clothes there. I resented it because Tatay made the well without their help. We couldn't take our clothes off when we washed at the well because sometimes they came unannounced.

Later, Tatay buried a long steel pipe and installed a water pump at the back of our house. The water well he had dug was then used for watering the nearby vegetable plants. It was dangerous to scoop water from the well, especially when the level of water was deep. It only overflowed when it rained so usually we had to bend down to scoop the water. The water pump was a better option. It was hard for me to pump because I was tiny but despite the difficulty, it was better than carrying a heavy pail of water.

Tatay was always full of ideas. In addition to the water pump, he made a huge water tank to catch the rain coming from the gutter of the roof of our house. He took a huge gasoline tank, elevated on a plank with stairwell, so it would be easy for him to see how much water was left. He placed a tap at the bottom of the tank to fill our water containers. This water was used for laundry, water for the animals, and miscellaneous needs. We were never allowed to go up the stairs to the water tank for fear we might drown. Tatay placed a very thin cloth like a sieve on top of the water tank and covered it with a lid. Mosquito net was a good material to use as a sieve. We used mosquito nets during the night because the mosquitoes were large, and we got itchy when we were bitten. Sometimes the scars from our scratching would take months to heal.

We loved having a bath when it rained. It was fun to go out in the rain. It was even more fun when we stood under the gutter to enjoy the full downpour of the rainwater on our heads and bodies. We squealed with delight while jumping and playing around. It was a lovely experience as a child!

Chapter 4

The three of us elder siblings were very close. We played together and shared adventures, exploring our surroundings. We found fish from the creek below the main road and bird nests with eggs in the rice paddies. We used slingshots to topple clusters of raw mangoes in the old mango tree that had grown tall and hard to climb.

When Nanay was busy with her chores, Ate Vernie took me to the fields. She picked ears of corn, chopped ripe bananas and dug kamote (sweet potatoes). She boiled all these in a pot suspended by a long sturdy stick on top of a fire of logs and twigs. While waiting for the food to cook, we talked about our adventures and the next one she planned. I had to keep these escapades a secret from our parents, otherwise I wouldn't be included. When the food was cooked, we ate with relish until we had our fill. Ate Vernie poured water onto the burning fire to smother the embers, then she collected our things to head home. My elder sister was only two years older than me but mature for her age. Nanay didn't have to worry about us when she was busy because we were self-sufficient and had the resourcefulness to feed ourselves.

I loved hanging out with Ate Vernie and Kuya Tito because they were fun to be with. Ate Vernie, was resourceful, gutsy and adventurous. Their escapades were usually dangerous and they got punished sometimes because they were so naughty. Tatay didn't punish me because I did as I was told. I was always in trouble with my siblings though, because they thought I dobbed them in. I didn't but Tatay always found out about their mischief.

We were a great team. The best experience I had with Kuya and Ate was when the rice fields were flooded. I'm not sure if the flood was caused by a typhoon or the monsoon rains that occurred regularly in the Philippines. The monsoons started as early as May and continued up to August or even November. When the rain went on for days, the rice fields got flooded. The bananas, bamboos and other tall trees were the only ones standing. After being cooped up in the house for so long, we got bored. My brother and sister saw the aftermath of the flood as a chance to use their ingenuity, creative and adventurous talents.

After the flood, Kuya Tito and Ate Vernie chopped the fallen banana trees and made a raft by tying the trunks together with strong vines and rope from the house. The raft was crudely bound, but good enough to ride like a floating barge along the flooded fields. My brother and sister really had guts. I just observed and watched in amazement. I wondered how they could create such a wonderful craft. At first I was scared to join them because I couldn't swim. They learnt to swim without anyone teaching them. They waded through the waters without fear as if it was a natural thing to do. When I fell into the water, they had to rescue me. I guess

I was a liability to them but because they loved me, they let me tag along. I joined them on the makeshift raft, having the thrill of getting up and down the raft despite sliding into the water several times. It was great fun to float along the flooded rice fields.

Kuya Tito and Ate Vernie's next adventure was even more daring. They hid on the side of the street at night to wait for the truck full of harvested sugar cane that came from the upper barrio Tuburan. I tagged along despite my fears. My role was to collect the pieces of sugar cane they dropped from the truck and hide them on the side of the street. The aim was to get as many as we could from a moving truck stacked with freshly harvested sugar cane. They only did this when there was no moon. The trucks loaded with sugar cane passed by around 9 or 10 in the evening on a pitch black night.

The trucks came from the upper barrio, a few kilometres away. Barrio Tuburan had hectares and hectares of sugar cane plantations. Trucks came to and from there at night to pick up the harvest to be processed in town. Kuya Tito and Ate Vernie discovered this and it gave them the idea for their daring adventure. They plotted a way to get the most succulent and juicy sugar canes you could imagine. Kuya Tito and Ate Vernie somehow knew the schedule of the cane trucks and how many would pass during the night. If other trucks were coming later, they would wait until the last one passed before they executed their daring act. It would be a disaster if they were seen pulling the sugar canes by another truck coming from behind. I was in awe of my elder siblings because they were so clever, courageous and fearless. As part of the team, I was compelled to assist them.

The time came and I was nervous but they said if I didn't join in, I wouldn't get a share. That shot my adrenalin to a full pitch of bravery. I went with them to the road to wait for the trucks to pass by. My siblings allotted enough time for us to hide in the dark. I was shaky and almost in tears because it was dark and I was afraid of any sound. There might be snakes or witches around. When we heard the sound of an engine from the bridge, I was told to be quiet. We could see the headlights. The truck was running very slowly due to the weight of its load. We could even hear the creaking when the truck swayed on the road. It must have been travelling at a speed of 10–20 kilometres per hour. Four trucks passed that night. When the last truck passed our hiding place, Kuya Tito and Ate Vernie ran behind the truck and pulled out long sugar canes one after the other from the stack in the truck. Because the truck moved slowly, they pulled as much as they could until they got tired and thought that we had enough for the night. I picked up the canes that fell on the road and hid them on the side of the road. It was also my role to signal them if someone was coming. When Kuya Tito and Ate Vernie came back after running for around half a kilometre, they helped me pick up the canes and we all carried them home. I was tiny so it was hard for me but I couldn't complain. If I did, I wouldn't get a share. It was even harder for Kuya and Ate as they carried the heaviest load.

Our hard work was repaid by a joyful feast in front of the bonfire when we got home. Ate and Kuya removed the leaves from the top end of the sugar cane with a hacking knife. They cut each long cane into five or six portions. We removed the hard skin of the sugar cane with our teeth and bit the soft part, munching and sucking the fresh juice. We call it pangos.

I came to learn that we were in luck if the sugar cane was the soft, bigger, reddish type because it was juicier and softer. If the load happened to be the long, thin, greenish ones, we didn't have much fun because they were hard to munch. My elder siblings would chop off the hard skin first before giving us our portions. After we finished sucking the juice from the soft part of the cane, we spat it out, and bit more from our cut portion. We could take another cut if we wanted. We did this until we got tired of munching or we were just too tired.

The big, reddish sugar canes were processed into raw sugar and molasses. We loved molasses because it was sticky and sweet and known for its beneficial effects. I think molasses was also fed to the horses. We also learned that munching sugar cane was good exercise for the jaw and the teeth. We didn't even have to brush our teeth as the sugar cane fibre cleaned them.

Chapter 5

The men in the community have their own pastime. They raised roosters and honed their fighting skills for sabong (cockfighting). The chickens' feet were fitted with razors or tightly-tied nails. When the sabong started, the men placed bets on their favourite chicken. When the fighting was really intense, you could hear excited male voices reverberating all over the fields. These chickens fought to the death. Sometimes the opponent was badly wounded when the game was over. If a chicken died, it became a pulutan or savoury dish for the men to eat while drinking tuba, a fermented coconut wine. The cockfights usually took place near the main road. A hut was built with an elevated viewing area for observers to sit or stand on while watching the chickens fight on the ground arena.

We children had our own ways of entertaining ourselves. Nanay and Tatay normally let us explore the fields nearby. Most of the time we went together for our adventures, but there were times when Kuya wanted to be with other boys in the neighbourhood. Then, Ate Vernie would lead our exploration. Ate Vernie always took a hacking knife wherever we went. She chopped off thorns and vines that flapped across our faces when we walked along the bushy areas. We found wild red berries along the way. We knew which ones were poisonous. If we found bird nests containing eggs in the rice paddies, we loved taking them home to be boiled for a particularly delicious snack.

Our favourite tree was the camachile tree. The fruit of the camachile was curled like the first quarter of the moon. We knew when they were ripe because the skin broke, showing the white flesh inside. The seed made it tedious to eat. You had to break it open, like peeling peas. The fruit was sweet when ripe but sometimes tasted bland. If we couldn't reach the camachile fruits, we used a long stick to bend the branch.

My favourite toy was the slingshot. We made our own out of a sturdy Y-shaped twig and a thick rubber. The old mango tree down from the house was tall and massive. I couldn't climb its trunk to get to the branches with fruit, so a slingshot was useful. I also tried shooting at birds in the trees. The birds flew away fast when startled so I never managed to hit one.

We also played with yoyos and spinning tops. I was not very good at these games and I thought of them as boys' games. I tried the hula hoop but I always dropped it without having it roll over my hips, so I gave that up.

My favourite game was chato, a stick game made out of short and long sticks. The short stick was wedged horizontally against two stones. We scooped it up with the long stick, hit it hard when it was up in the air and let it fly as far as possible. If our opponent caught it, we were dead, and it was the other player's turn.

We also had a game called piko or skip, hop and step. We drew a big square line on the soil with an oval circle on top called the home run. We then drew horizontal lines that touched each end of the square, and then cut them into portion of squares to jump and step in. The farther we threw our pato, a flat thin stone, to mark our territorial space, the more squares we could hop and step. We selected the pato from the slimmest, flattest stones we could find in the river or on the street. Our pato had to land inside the square, otherwise we were out and the next player took over. We closed our eyes when we jumped between squares and had to shout 'Step?/No?' to find out whether or not we were safely inside the square. We did this until we finished the squares and landed on the home run. Whoever jumped on the most squares up to the home base won. If anyone stepped on the line, they were dead and the next player had their turn. We played this game at night, especially when there was a full moon.

We had another game called sipa, which means kick. We covered a coin with a thin cloth bundled at the top with a thread or a rubber band. We kicked it with the flat of our inside or outside shin. The shin gave it a nice bounce, so we could kick again and again until we dropped it. We also had skipping ropes, ran our own marathon races, and played various ball games. We usually played hide and seek during full moon so our parents wouldn't worry about us playing outside. The hardest playmates to find were those who hid on top of the roof of our house, and those outside the fields far away from where we had a home start.

We made our own toys out of materials we could get hold of, so we improvised. I remember the doll I made out of calico from Nanay's sewing. I drew the face with red crayon for the lips and I finished off by embroidering the features. I also made a playhouse out of twigs and sticks, tied with ropes and vines. The roof was made of wide banana leaves and the flooring of dried cogon grass I gathered from the fields. It was good fun because I could lie down and eat lollies, boiled corn or bananas inside my little playhouse. When the roof of the playhouse collapsed due to the crude way it was made, it spoiled my fun and I threw a tantrum.

I loved touching the makahiya (touch-me-not) weeds that grew freely in the fields on dry land near our house. When you touched the leaves, they closed up and if you swept your hand across them, the leaves closed in sequence like magic. It had thorns, though, so if you weren't careful, you could get pricked.

There was a season when big dragonflies flew freely in the fields. Hundreds of them flew and their different colours were lovely. We used to chase and capture insects and put them in a bottle. The dragonflies and grasshoppers were big, the beetles were dark brown. Some were small, some were big.

Different kinds of spiders cast their webs on walls and sometimes in the rice fields. There were also swarms of bees but we shied away from them as one time, we accidentally disturbed a beehive and were bitten. Nanay had to administer first aid with plant juice – a green thick plant which I think was aloe vera.

There were times when we climbed fruit trees and found caterpillars crawling on the leaves. I was told that these caterpillars produced beautiful butterflies. At first, I saw them in cocoons. When they emerged as caterpillars and moved on the leaves with their many tiny feet, I was scared and disgusted. But when I saw a beautiful, multi-coloured butterfly flying, I began to appreciate where they came from – those cocoons and those caterpillars. I loved hunting butterflies. They were elusive and always settled on the higher leaves beyond our reach. For our class experiment, we caught butterflies to preserve and display in an album. Their coloured wings were a beauty to behold.

The major preoccupation of Kuya Tito and his playmates was gathering different kinds of beetles and placing them in bottles or boxes. They put the beetles on the floor or a wooden table and let them fight. My eldest brother always captured the strong ones. His beetles won most of the time. It fascinated me to watch these little insects biting one another.

When our first cousins from Iloilo City came to visit us at the farm, it was always a big event. We were a close-knit family and because we seldom saw each other, we made up for lost time. The most hilarious experience I had with them was when we all rode the back of the carabao. Kuya Tito was at the helm near the carabao's head, controlling the rope tied to its nose. Next was Ate Beth, the daughter of my father's sister. She was older than Kuya Tito. Then came Ate Vernie and I was last. The carabao must have been uncomfortable with all of us little rascals climbing on its back. It suddenly flicked us off, making us fall, sliding backwards. Because I was the last in the queue, I was thrown off first into the mud, followed by everyone else. We were on top of each other in the muddy rice field. We were covered with mud, but we found it hilarious. Nanay was not amused when she saw our dishevelled appearance. We were ordered to clean ourselves right away and told never to do it again. Did you think we cared? Nah! We all laughed and giggled. We'd had the most fun in our life, mud and all.

In the evening, we lit bonfires and talked animatedly about anything we could think of. Ate Beth was the giggly one. We always laughed at her funny stories. She had a great sense of humour and found something funny in almost anything. She made stories out of what she observed. During these bonfires, we tossed the newly picked ears of corn, bananas, sweet potatoes and cashew nuts into the burning charcoal.

The cashew nuts produced an aroma which filled our senses and the air around us with its sweet roasting smell. When the food was cooked, we enjoyed a hearty meal. We were allowed to stay up late, so we made the most of it.

I spent one unforgettable day with my well-to-do uncle. Ate Vernie, my cousin Antoinette and I were invited to spend a weekend in Iloilo City where my bachelor uncle Isidro lived. We called him Tay Idring. He was an accountant by profession and being single, was more affluent than his siblings.

Tay Idring took us around town on a shopping spree. We went to a clothing material shop in Iloilo City as a treat and he let us choose material we liked. Each one of us had our own favourites, but my uncle, being wise as well as generous, ordered a pretty dainty-coloured material, enough to make dresses for the three of us. Then he brought us to the dressmaker to be measured. The three of us ended with puffed-sleeved dresses with a ribbon at the back – very pretty, but we all had the same material and styles. We looked like triplets in uniform.

Chapter 6

There came a time when an infestation of locusts swarmed our rice fields without warning. They made the sky dark. We heard the terrifying sound of their buzzing when they passed through. We closed the doors, windows and holes in the walls to stop them entering the house. I didn't know the significance of this event until Tatay told us that all the rice had been destroyed by the hordes of locusts. All that was left in the rice fields were stalks.

Tatay was devastated because almost the whole crop of rice was gone. We were lucky that some fields not directly in the path of the swarming locusts were salvaged. It was also the first time I'd ever tasted fried locusts. Tatay fried the ones that dropped in the rice paddies like dried anchovies. Although it was weird and scary to eat them first, they actually tasted good. Tatay said there was no harm eating them as they only ate leaves or grains of rice where they passed through.

I was around nine years old when Tatay stopped farming. I don't know whether this was the aftermath of locust infestation or because of the hardship of the farming life. At the time my focus was on school. I was nearing my primary school graduation and vying for honours with my two male classmates. As long as my parents were around, I was happy.

Our new source of livelihood was a dry goods business in town that Tatay bought. When he came back home in the evenings, he always brought us treats like lollies and fresh bread. He never failed to bring a bag of goodies or food for the family. He usually arrived late in the afternoon or at night in time for dinner. We were always excited when he came home because it meant we had pasalubongs or treats from Tatay.

At the end of the week, he also brought our favourite magazine written in both the native dialect and the Filipino language. This was how I learned our national language at a young age. On weekends, Kuya Tito, Ate Vernie and I went to town to help Tatay sell goods from our stall. It was a new experience and it also gave us the opportunity to earn rewards for our hard work – usually lollies and goods that we coveted for ourselves.

Chapter 7

My grandfather had a big influence on my childhood memories. We called him Lolo Dikoy, but his name was Federico. Nanay's father lived with us on the farm after my grandmother passed away.

Lolo Dikoy used to climb coconut trees with his bolo (scythe). He tied a big bag to his waist before climbing the tree. He had already chopped wedges on the side of the coconut trees to step on as he climbed, aided by a long rope. He did this very early in the morning and when he came back, he had a jarful of tuba, fresh, warm coconut juice ready to drink. I was curious so I asked Lolo Dikoy where he got this tuba. He said that he cut the core on the very top of the tree. When it was cut, fresh coconut liquid oozed and poured into his bamboo tube. When it was finished, he slid down the coconut tree.

Nanay drank this tuba after giving birth to my younger siblings. Before drinking it, she added one freshly hatched chicken egg, squeezed calamansi juice from the Filipino lime, stirred it well and drank it immediately. Nanay told me it sustained and gave her strength for a fast recovery after childbirth. I tasted the tuba and liked it but I was cautioned not to drink too much as it would make me drunk. I now realise that the drink was the equivalent of malted beer. If the tuba was not finished during the day, it was left to ferment for a few days until it turned into vinegar. Nanay used this to cook pork adobo or fish.

Lolo Dikoy grew his own tobacco crop in one of Tatay's fields on the southwest side of our land. Our rice fields were on the east. He planted the tobacco plants in a rich moist soil and watered them religiously, row by row, until they grew tall and had wide healthy leaves. Then he harvested them and let us help him secure the hand-picked leaves on a long pole. He hung these long poles filled with wide tobacco leaves in rows, on a roofed shed that he built himself, until they dried. When the tobacco leaves were thoroughly dried, he placed them in sacks and took them to sell at the market in town. He showed us how to make a cigar out of the tobacco leaves. When he finished, he lit one of the rolled and folded tobacco leaves and smoked it with relish. It produced a fresh pungent smell. I wasn't sure how he bartered or traded the tobacco. All I knew was that my Lolo worked painstakingly on his tobacco plantation to earn money for himself. We relished helping him as he bought us goodies when he sold his tobacco – cookies, lollies, and sometimes a dress for me and my sister.

It's a pity that I have few memories of my grandparents on Nanay's side. The only thing I remember about my grandmother was seeing her lying in bed when she was sick. I was very young then and scared to go near her. When she passed away, I was dressed up to attend her funeral. My grandfather was a good-looking man with a beautiful high-bridged nose. My mother's good looks must have come from him. The surname Bernil had a tint of Spanish, a relic of three centuries of Spanish colonisation.

I saw several unusual occurrences during my childhood. Sometime in the 1950s, I remember Nanay rousing us from our sleep around 2 am. She told us that we had to see a comet because it was an exceptional phenomenon. My siblings and I didn't know what she meant but when we went outside the house, we understood. Without the aid of telescope, we looked up to the clear sky towards the east and saw up above in the clear sky, a huge comet with a long tail like a broom. It was so big and bright that in a child's eye, it was magnificent. It gave me the shivers. It was a vision that was awesome! We were told it only appeared in the sky every hundred years and if I heard it right, the long sweeping tail was an omen of difficult years ahead.

It had become a family routine that when the sky was clear at night, Nanay would gaze up to the sky and tell us about the galaxy. We listened in awe as she pointed to the North and the South Stars, the Three Kings, Noah's Ark, the Evening Star, and other stars in the Milky Way. Years later when we lived in Sydney I asked Nanay how she knew about these things. She had no formal schooling and her life revolved around the family. We were chatting as we often did about the family, life, the past, the here and now. She explained that she read, listened to the news on the radio and talked to the neighbours about unusual occurrences.

I was always amazed by my mother's wisdom and knowledge. She read, wrote and understood English well. She read magazines, the *Sydney Morning Herald* and other newspapers without the aid of eyeglasses. When she read, she was truly engrossed. Afterwards during our casual conversations, she would comment about what was happening around the world and what she had read or seen on television. Nanay had a knack of observing things in her own quiet way.

When we were young, Nanay told us stories about the Japanese occupation – how they hid and fled from advancing Japanese soldiers. She told us an unusual story about the small bridge above a narrow stream near where we lived. It was the bridge where people crossed to go to the next barrio, Tuburan. Both sides had tall bamboos with leaves almost obscuring the view of what was ahead of that bridge. I was scared to cross the bridge even with friends. Nanay said that on that bridge, the soldiers snatched small children from their mother's arms, threw them up in the air, caught with bayonets and dropped them in the stream to die. They then raped the women and killed them.

There were occasions when we heard horrific moans and saw a rolling ball of fire from our balcony. We called this santilmo in our dialect. It came from a path where there was a tree at the corner of the road. It happened when it was drizzling on a dark night. We cowered in fright because it sounded and looked scary. When we asked Nanay what it was, she said that it must have been the unblessed souls of those who died during the war needing prayers. Many soldiers and civilians were killed during the Japanese occupation in the area.

Nanay told me that before we lived in the barrio, I had the ability to see and feel a presence. One night while she was cooking dinner, she heard me scream. She ran to find out what it was. I pointed to the corner of the house and said that someone was there. Nanay took her hacking bolo and chopped at the unseen presence. When it moved around the house, I pointed to each place and Nanay followed and hacked at the place without seeing anything. This was before we moved to the house that Tatay built. It must have been my grandparents' house because when my grandmother died, my grandfather, Lolo Federico, came to live with us on the farm.

We were devout Catholics and Nanay always inculcated in us the moral values handed down from generation to generation. We always went to Sunday mass. We siblings didn't mind walking a few kilometres because it meant dressing up in our best clothes and socialising with the community. The mass was always said in Latin. Even though I didn't understand a word of Latin, I followed the prayers easily because I loved the roll of Latin on my tongue. Ultimately, I was able to say the *Pater Noster* (Our Father), *Ave Maria*, the Latin songs, the litanies, and the *Ora pro nobis*. I loved the lace veils girls and ladies wore inside church. We had long black, white or cream lace veils to cover our heads and shoulders. As a younger girl, I was given a round veil just to cover my head, secured by hairpins. As well as Sunday mass, we also said morning and evening prayers and the Angelus at 6 pm.

There was a time when Aunt Natividad, Nanay's elder sister, took me to her place in town to stay with her as a companion because she lived alone in her house. She was stricter than my mother and we had to say the Holy Rosary and the long litanies every day. My role was to answer the litanies with *Ora pro nobis, Amen, Mea culpa*. At one of our ritual prayers, I got so bored that I just bolted out. I was usually obedient but I was a child and I wanted to play. When my aunt noticed no one was answering her litanies, she called my name in a loud and menacing voice and I knew I was in big trouble. I was pinched hard as a punishment. I had to be obedient during prayer times and could only play outside after prayers. It was hard when the prayers were so long. If I said 'leche', which meant milk in Spanish but could be a form of a mild swearing, I was punished. Although my aunt sounds austere and strict, she spoilt me, giving me everything I could wish for – pretty clothes, food, lollies and a lot of cuddles.

I'll never forget a hilarious incident when I was staying with my aunt. Like my parents, she raised her own chickens. One day, she asked me to help her hold the chicken she was preparing for a chicken casserole. I knew how a chicken was killed; the throat was cut and then it was dipped into boiling water to remove the feathers before it was cut into pieces for cooking. The chicken wriggled in my hands while she was doing this, so I let go. It flopped off the open veranda where my aunt was working and she had to go down and finish the job. She was angry with me but I refused to help her. I felt sorry for the chicken. Which child would not?

Chapter 8

When I was four and a half years old I almost died of tosperina (whooping cough). It happened after a merry-go-round ride during our town fiesta. I was thrilled during the ride but in the evening, I developed a very high fever and was taken to a doctor in town when my fever didn't subside. I had spasms of coughing and my discharges were alarming. Nanay and Tatay carried me in their arms to town regularly for my injection. I was scared of needles, and I always cried when injected. I couldn't eat anything. Tatay bought Valencia oranges and squeezed the juice into my mouth so I would be nourished. Imported oranges were expensive but my father always bought them to sustain me as it seemed to be the only thing I could take. Nanay crushed the leaves of amargoso (bitter gourd) and mixed it with red sugar. She let me drink it, undiluted, by the spoonful.

While I was convalescing, my father brought me to Iloilo City where his family lived. He took me to Guimaras, a beautiful island. Tatay hired a canoe and brought me to the sea every day, so I could inhale fresh ocean air. It was said that sea salt had a therapeutic effect and would be good for my lungs. Tatay was very patient and gave me tender loving care until I got well.

After I recovered, I got bored at home and wasn't interested in playing on my own. I wanted to go to school too like my eldest brother and sister. I was four and a half years old but the school wouldn't enrol me until I was five. There was no kindergarten. I persevered until I was allowed to attend as an observing pupil. The school was more than a kilometre from our house, but the walk was good for me. It made me well and strong.

My primary school days were memorable, providing perspective on my later life. I did well in class and always enjoyed school. I loved the challenge of competing with my classmates. I was a well-groomed child who spoke her mind. Some of my teachers scooped me up in their arms when I was new in school. My classmates loved pinching me on both cheeks. I had chubby cheeks. I hated that because it hurts. There were no school uniforms but I went to school with ironed clothes, beautifully combed hair tied with ribbons and I wore wooden sandals or shoes because I refused to walk on the dirt road or dry rice paddies without shoes.

I started representing our school in declamation contests when I was around seven years old. These were competitions held between schools in different barrios. My first declamation was entitled 'Three Sisters Plus One Rocking Chair'. It started like this:

Mr Alcott had just started sitting down to his desk when he heard loud and angry voices in the next room. 'Give it to me. Give it to me… Give… it to me.'

It was about three sisters bickering over the one rocking chair in the house. It has been a long time since I delivered the declamation, but I still remember the opening words. My English teacher coached me on how to enact the scenes and speak the different voices of Mr Alcott and his three daughters. In declamation, we delivered our oratory with emphatic actions and tones to portray the different emotions of the characters. In this instance, it was the angry emotions of the three sisters fighting to possess that rocking chair. Mr Alcott was very cool in handling his bickering daughters. I can't remember how it ended, but it earned an outburst of applause from the audience. I won the declamation contest which was an honour for Madong Elementary School.

Representing the school as a declaimer was hard work because on top of my studies, my English teacher, Mrs Cadete, took me to her big house in Janiuay on weekends to practise my piece at every opportunity, day and night. To my child's eyes, her family were well-off. Their house was big. They had a piano. The food and the bed where I slept were great compared with our humble food and abode. At that time, we five brothers and sisters shared a room, we slept on floor mats, and shared one or two blankets between us.

My teacher's daughter, Bernadette, studied in an exclusive girls' school in town. She played the piano very well. During my time, only well-to-do people could afford a piano, so I felt privileged staying with them. Bernadette became my friend. One time, she gave me lollies to share during our girly night chats. This wasn't a good idea though, as my teacher was a disciplinarian and I was strictly forbidden candy or sweets. When she caught me with a candy in my mouth, I was told to spit it out and was given a big chunk of raw ginger instead. This had to stay in my mouth overnight. She said it would ensure that my voice would be full, firm and clear. This was a regimen especially one day prior to the declamation contest.

Mrs Cadete checked me at night to ensure that the ginger was still in my mouth.

It must have worked because my voice was clear, impressive and full when I delivered my piece. I was strictly supervised until the day of the competition and my clothes, hair and shoes were examined for perfection. My delivery and performance were thoroughly checked, and I was told that I should be confident in order to win. I obeyed because I was scared of punishment, be it from parents or teachers. I was a teacher's pet which made my classmates envious of me. As a school declaimer, my clothes were always of the best material, tailored just for me. I remember a baby pink dress and the pale lemon dress with faintly embossed patterns. They were so pretty that I felt like a princess, especially after they had done my hair and makeup. I was chauffeured to declamation places at the nearby barrios in a car.

I won for the school for almost two years before I came second to a declaimer from another school. That ended my career. I didn't get any more hand-made clothes of beautiful material in baby pink or pale lemon. I was back to ordinary clothes but I still felt privileged because Tatay bought me pretty dresses. It was a pity that my parents didn't have a camera then.

When I was a school declaimer, two of my classmates were my admirers. One of them was Bede, who even went on foot to follow our vehicle to the next barrio where the declamation contest was held. I liked him better than Nonito, the good-looking one who belonged to a well-off family in the barrio. Both of them were rascals though. One time, they cornered me in the school room for a kiss. I was very quick with my reflexes and I pushed them hard, so they ended up wedged on the wall. Bede was behind Nonito. He was pinned to the wall by a protruding nail. It wounded him and created a three-cornered tear on his shirt. As punishment, I was asked to sew the tear on his shirt. I cried because I didn't know how to sew. I asked my mother to sew it for me, but she refused. She connived with my teacher and admonished me because I hurt Bede's back with a wound from the nail. I cried and sulked for a week until the torn shirt was ultimately sewn by Nanay. I apologised for hurting Bede but told all of them that it was not my fault. I was still petulant. I caught my teacher and Nanay looking at each other, smiling.

I was active in most school activities. During our flag ceremony in the morning, I was in front of the class to lead the national anthem while the more senior class raised the flag. As a sign of reverence, we were required to place our right hand over our left chest while singing loudly. The boys were required to have their right hand on their foreheads as a gesture of salute. During that time, we had two national anthems and two flagpoles. We first sang the 'Star-Spangled Banner' while raising the American flag, then the 'Bayang Magiliw' or 'Land of the Morning', our Filipino national anthem, while the Filipino flag was raised. I understood later that we raised the American flag first because of our allegiance to them for liberating us from Japanese occupation, then we raised our national flag as a symbol of our national independence. I learned how to fold a flag after the ceremony. There were usually four of us holding each edge of the flag. We folded it in turns until it was reduced into a small triangular form. Then we reverently placed it in a drawer. It was a rule that the flag should never touch the ground.

Arbor Day was the first of May and we celebrated it every year. It was our custom to plant a tree on the day, so we planted one tree in front of our schoolyard. Our books were bilingual – English and Filipino. We had English and Filipino teachers. Our major curriculum subjects were English, Filipino, mathematics, physical education and home economics. I did well in everything except home economics. Once, my teacher pinched me because I made a mess in cooking. Most of the time, I didn't listen. I was easily distracted because cooking was not one of my favourite subjects. To be more attentive in class, Mrs Quintilla (a relative of my classmate Nonito), assigned me to be the ambassadress of the home economics department. I took samples of a cooked dish or a delicacy for the other teachers to taste and relayed their feedback to the home economics teacher.

I couldn't graduate without passing home economics, so I tried harder. I learned to embroider, which I loved, and also studied tatting, crocheting, sewing and cooking. I wasn't keen on sewing because I was impatient when threads tangled. I used to rip them apart or cut them and started all over again, sometimes in tears. I also didn't like washing up because I often broke things and got into trouble. I didn't mind cooking except that sometimes I got burnt or the food didn't taste good. I loved watching my classmates cook. In the end, I learned how to cook simple delicacies. My favourite was the teatime delicacy, palitaw. I perfected the art of dropping the moulded rice balls into boiling water until they floated. They tasted good dipped in sugar with sesame seeds and coconut flakes. I learned to fry sesame seeds without burning them and how to grate fresh mature coconut. Our graters were small round tins imbedded in a long piece of wood. We sat on the long wood while grating the halved coconut. The sesame seeds, raw sugar and freshly grated coconut were important ingredients to sprinkle over the top of the cooked palitaw to give it a yummy taste, a good afternoon snack to fill a hungry stomach.

During our primary grades we had rations of Hemo Bordens, a chocolate drink like Milo and Klim, Dutch powdered milk. We would line up to get our rations and also for a spoonful of cod liver oil. I disliked the taste and smell of it. We were told to pinch our noses to swallow. We were also required to have immunisations – measles, diphtheria and smallpox. The dotted smallpox injection was painful. It was supposed to swell and leave a scar mark on the upper arm. I didn't have a scar, so I wondered if it had worked on me.

We were also purged once a year to get rid of worms. I hated it. It was crude and uncomfortable. They used a tube to insert into our anus and pumped in the water to fill our stomach from the contents of the labatiba (a big water bag) with medication. Afterwards we had no choice but to go to the toilet. Our parents administered this, and we were all monitored in one big house near the school which belonged to the Layadors, my classmate Bede's parents. They had a lounge room big enough for most of us classmates who lived far from school. After our ordeal, we weren't allowed to eat anything except rice porridge without anything in it but a pinch of salt.

At school we made a cardboard sundial and learnt to tell the time by the position of the sun. The long and short dials were pinned by thumb tacks on the cardboard. When the sun's shadow fell onto the sundial, we could tell what time it was. Now, in an age of technology, I don't know how to position a sundial anymore. During an eclipse, we were taught how to shade a piece of flat glass with fire smoke that blackened the glass. We looked through this to view the eclipse. We also became scouts and knew how to place a tourniquet on a wound to stop bleeding and how to build a fire without a match. We did this by positioning a magnifying glass so that the heat of the sun could burn a mound of dry leaves below stacked sticks.

Our teachers were great! Miss Havana was my teacher in Grade 1, Mrs Domello in Grade 2 and of course Mrs Cadete, my English teacher in Grade 3 who taught me how to be a school declaimer. There was also Miss Braga who was fastidious in the way she dressed. She spoke eloquently and used her hands to express her point. Our mathematics teacher was good but strict. She would smack us on our hands with a ruler if she caught us counting with our fingers. We were told to use our brains. She made us memorise our multiplication tables and recite them in class every day. This method worked very well because I can still multiply without using a calculator.

I am including this event because it was one of my momentous accomplishments when I was young. I was six years old when I became second in the Miss Stamp contest in Tara-Tara, a few kilometres away from Madong. I have a faint memory of my father putting me on his shoulders when we crossed several rivers on our way to that distant barrio. We had several suitcases of stamps on the wooden tray of the cartwheel that carried our things. They were to be counted for the Miss Stamp competition. I also knew there was a beautiful dress for me in one of those suitcases. I was told that I could have won the competition except that the parents of the winner threatened violence if their daughter did not win. My father had more suitcases of stamps to be counted but they hid them to prevent any trouble.

Many years later, I was surprised when Nanay showed me a picture during one of my homecoming visits from Taipei, Taiwan, where I worked. We were talking about our life in the barrio when Nanay took out this picture from her files.

It was taken during the Miss Stamp competition. I was really touched to see myself as a small girl dressed in a gala gown with a handsome consort, my cousin. I didn't know I looked so cute then! I was thankful that my parents had arranged for this picture to be taken by a professional photographer. I took it, along with others, when we migrated to Australia. It was one of the few mementoes of my childhood.

Miss Stamp runner-up, Nora on the left

Chapter 9

Kuya Tito, Ate Vernie and I excelled in our studies and we were always on the honour roll. They graduated ahead of me but during school ceremony awards, our surname was always called. My eldest brother Tito was a salutatorian, my elder sister Veronica, a valedictorian, and myself, a salutatorian. I ran second to Nonito, our valedictorian. Earlier, Bede and I tied but I beat him as salutatorian in our final year. He became the first honourable mention. Through the years until we graduated from primary school, Nonito, Bede and I remained good friends.

During our graduation, we presented a drama where I was the Goddess of Wisdom. I wore a white dress, a tiara and a white magic wand, all made by Nanay. Some of my classmates played drug addicts. We used multi-coloured lollies as drugs placed in different bottles. My classmates took some lollies from the bottles, swayed and dropped to the floor. I spoke my lines and waved my magic wand to make them well. I didn't understand anything about drugs and why we were depicting that episode in our drama. It was all foreign to me yet my speech was full of wisdom, as I waved my wand over the addicts to make them well and free from evil spirits. Perhaps it was taken from the movie, *Valley of the Dolls*. It was around then that drugs came into our awareness.

We also presented a dance performance. I loved the dance Point Your Little Foot because it was the first time I ever danced properly with a male partner. We girls had black taffeta blouses and a mix of fuchsia and black crepe paper sewn together as a skirt. While we were waiting for our turn to dance, we roamed around the flower gardens. My skirt got caught in the thorns of a rose bush. I knew I was in trouble because the crepe material was torn, and my skirt drooped. It looked uneven and awful, so I asked a friend to cut off the torn portion. It made my skirt shorter than intended, but nobody seemed to notice.

Among my best childhood memories was my primary education at Madong Elementary School. It gave me the opportunity to compete and excel in class, to represent our school as a declaimer, and to be recognised in our barrio as one of the top students in school. I followed the footsteps of my elder siblings Kuya Tito and Ate Vernie and I was happy with my accomplishments.

I kept some beautiful samples of my embroidery in primary grades, but when I came back to the Philippines from Taipei, all my mementoes were gone. Even the special white baby jacket of my first-born son and my diaries of his first words, first haircut and other beautiful memories. I was sentimental about my treasured things but the people I trusted to live in my house didn't care. Luckily I saved a few old pictures and my university degree before we moved to Australia. Some were taken at the house where I grew up – Kuya Tito and Ate Vernie feeding the chickens, a family picture with our beloved dog Brownie in front of the house, and a picture of me when I was around five years old. These were treasured memories of my childhood and the old big house that Tatay built.

Feeding chickens in our farm

In front of original house - (L-R) me, Kuya Tito, Nanay, Ate Vernie, Frank in front and our dog Brownie

Chapter 10

We moved to a new house sometime after I graduated from primary school. The new place was not in an open-spaced area like our old house. It was surrounded by bamboos in an enclosure that obscured the entrance and exit and hid our view to the fields. The yard was also smaller. I preferred the old house that Tatay built, with a ground floor and an upper floor, a huge balcony and several rooms. It had an unhindered view of the rice fields and the neighbourhood. I don't understand what happened or why we lost the old place. This house had been transported but only the main structure of the old house was moved so it would fit into a smaller space. The extensions of the old house were dismantled.

When we moved, it was through the Bayanihan system, a custom of helping one another in the community. The male neighbours uprooted the old house and carried it on their shoulders. They walked the distance in synchronised steps, with someone leading and shouting directions. When they reached the destination, they planted the house in holes that had been dug for the four corners of the house. At this time, houses were built with bamboo poles, bamboo floors and nipa thatched roofs.

I felt scared there because we were secluded. Our neighbour, who used to live in this area, had moved away. Here, the sound of lightning and thunderstorms reverberated and swirled, producing loud and horrifying bangs. The lightning cracked like explosions in the sky. When this happened, my siblings and I clustered together on a big mat on the bamboo floor. In our old house in the open field we hadn't been afraid. I was now the eldest in the family as Kuya Tito and Ate Vernie weren't living with us anymore. Again, I didn't understand why.

After we settled in this small house, I looked after my younger brothers and sister when Nanay and Tatay were away attending to our dry goods business in town. I grew up quickly because I was responsible for looking after my younger brothers and sister. I learned to build a fire, using dried grass to light it. I used chopped wood and cooked rice on a clay pot. I did all the household chores as we didn't have helpers anymore. I was around ten years old then.

One time, Nanay and Tatay came home late from business in town. I was scared because I heard a *tik, tik, tik* noise moving around the house. I'd heard stories that when a witch wanted to come inside the house to get small children, she created that sound in her excitement. I got hold of the big, long hacking knife and swished it around the area where the *tik, tik, tik* came from, to show I wasn't scared despite the thundering fear in my heart. My aim was to protect my younger brothers and sister. I placed one big mat on the floor and huddled them together. If an intruder was downstairs looking up at our floor, they wouldn't see us through the slits in the elevated bamboo flooring. Our walls were solid with no slits, so I concentrated on the floor because our windows were shut and locked. I relaxed when I heard Nanay and Tatay come home and call us before they got up the ladder of the house. I cried in relief as I had been very scared. There were no kidnappings or house invasions that we knew of then. The neighbours, all good people, were one or two kilometres away. All the people in the barrio knew and helped one another.

Every time my parents came home, they brought us treats. We always had good food, bread, lollies, new things for the house, and sometimes new clothes. All our fears vanished when we were lavished with so much love and affection. We hugged our parents and they in turn hugged and kissed each one of us. We always missed them, but we knew that they worked very hard to provide for us.

Later, Tatay moved his trade to Lambunao, a more distant town around an hour's travel by bus. Kuya Tito stayed there to mind our sari-sari (convenience) store so Tatay could come home on weekends. There were times when Nanay went there on weekdays and left me in charge of my younger siblings.

After Tatay's small business moved to Lambunao, I sensed that something went wrong. I began to notice that Tatay didn't come home as often as he used to. Nanay never complained or showed her heartache or difficulties. She was always there for us. If something was wrong, she didn't say. I never saw her cry or break down but I sensed trouble because we didn't have enough food or provisions. We must have been told that Tatay wasn't coming back anymore. I wondered why Kuya Tito and Ate Vernie lived in Iloilo with my well-off uncle. I had been young and happy when I graduated from primary school and what happened made me very sad. I thought my father was a good father because he was devoted to us at work and at play when we lived in the big house. He was the one who administered first aid when I stepped on a rusty nail. I used to make a pretend horse of him when I rode on his back at play when we all lived together.

Because of my father's absence, I knew I had to help Nanay feed my younger brothers and sister. I stopped going to school and I volunteered to help at home. I was told that Kuya Tito and Ate Vernie lived with my Uncle in Iloilo City because he got married and he needed helpers to run the household chores and ran errands. The three of us, Kuya Tito, Ate Vernie and I, have stopped going to school.

I learned later that Tatay left because he had a mistress. It broke my heart.

I looked for opportunities to help Nanay any way I could. When I heard from friends that a group of them were going to harvest rice, I volunteered to join them. A pretty lady called Jessica and the lad courting her led our group to the mountains. We crossed rivers and climbed mountains with our sack of clothes and things needed to harvest rice. It was difficult for me because I was little. The two adults in the group helped me when the path got steep, but it was all right when we reached the top landing. There were times when we passed through green forests and here we had to ask permission – tabi-tabi (meaning excuse me) – from the invisible creatures who owned the forests. When we needed to drink from the water pools, we made the sign of the cross and were extra careful not to disturb the serenity of the place before we scooped up the crisp, cool, water with our hands and filled our water jugs. We crossed seven rivers before we reached our destination. It seemed like forever. I was exhausted and wanted to cry because I was alone with strangers away from home, but I resolved to be brave and hide my tears.

Our arrival was expected and dinner was served when we arrived. It was a feast, with all kinds of delicacies and freshly prepared food. We drank fresh coconut milk and calamansi juice. We used a strainer to hold the calamansi seeds when we squeezed the juice into a jug of water, adding sugar to give it a tangy lemony taste.

After dinner, all I wanted to do was lie down in the shared room allocated to us. I was half-asleep when I heard the strumming of guitars and male voices singing outside the window. Jessica was being serenaded by her suitor, together with a group of male companions from the locality. It was a tradition to court a lady this way.

I found the serenade custom lovely but very old-fashioned. The lady had to pretend to be asleep before the serenade began. All the lights were put out. At that time, we used candles or oil lamps. When the young men came and started singing love songs to guitar accompaniment, the lady had to peep from the small opening of her thatched window at the men singing downstairs. It might take a while for her to open wide the window, so the men had to prepare several serenades. When she appeared at the window and recognised the serenaders, she had to ask our host's permission to invite them in. It was the custom to ask the couple who owned the place if the lady could let the suitor and his friends come up and talk to her. Usually, there was advance notice for this visit, so the host had prepared delicacies to serve the visitors. When the men were inside the house, the younger ones weren't allowed to sit with them – only the ladies of courting age, including the daughters of the house. The courting started with exchange of pleasantries like 'Kumusta ka?' (How are you?) or mano po, a customary sign of respect when the young men touched their forehead on the outstretched back hand of an elder. Introductions followed, then the man who fancied Jessica sat beside her. The others made small talk with our host to give the young couple a chance to talk privately. I observed this silent understanding that the man was given a chance to be seated next to his lady of interest so that they could exchange pleasantries in front of everyone. This courting session lasted until about midnight. We younger ones couldn't keep awake this long and sleep engulfed us before the much-coveted refreshments and delicacies were served. Usually the men were offered beer with home-made delicacies such as puto, suman and sapin-sapin.

The following day we woke early to have breakfast before going to the fields. We had fresh goat's milk and puto cooked on a charcoal fire. After breakfast, I was ready with my hat, a small hand scythe and a bag to start the new day harvesting rice on the mountain slope. The ladies and men were full of life and camaraderie, exchanging jokes, laughing and bantering. They alluded to the sweethearts in a joking manner. We were harvesting a beautiful variety of rice with long grains that smelled good and were soft when cooked. The rice stalks were tall, and the heavy grains of rice bent in one direction.

One hot and humid day when we were harvesting rice, clouds gathered and it rained heavily. We were caught by the downpour and decided to go back. Since we were all wet, we went to the river to wash our clothes. We laundered our clothes beside the river when we heard a loud roar upstream. A deluge of water was coming our way, taking everything in its path, including twigs and trees. I was mesmerised and stood still, watching the unfolding event. In the nick of time one of my companions snatched me from the river and dragged me to higher ground. I shivered in fright when I realised what could have happened if someone hadn't grabbed me. Afterwards, I stayed close to the group as I was shaken. They took turns looking after me. I cried that night, wishing I was with my mother and my family.

We stayed in that barrio for a couple of weeks before making our way home, taking the same path. It wasn't difficult on the way back even with the additional weight of our bundles of rice, payment for our hard work, because we were going downhill. We crossed the same forests and rivers. I took what I could carry in my knapsack as my share, four or five bundles of harvested rice.

It was a thrilling and unforgettable adventure, but I would never want to go through it again. When I reached home, I proudly showed Nanay my earnings. I didn't tell her about my harrowing experience in the river. I didn't want to add to her worries.

This experience taught me at a young age that earning a living meant determination, perseverance, hard work and taking risks. I cried but I resolved to be brave and to be there for my mother and younger brothers and sister.

The days turned into years with little hope for the future. Nanay, Kuya Tito, Ate Vernie and I were saddled with making a living. We didn't have time to dwell on our sorrows. After two years of hardship, something happened. We packed our bags and left our barrio, the place where I had spent my childhood. I was twelve years old.

The next thing I knew, we were waiting for a big ship bound for Manila to take us to an unknown future.

Chapter 11

It was only in 2013 at my younger brother Benjamin's wake, that I finally found out the truth about our family breakup. I went back to the Philippines when my brother died after a long illness. My first cousin Nonoy Boloy (his pet name) was there. He was a reliable source of information about family history, so I asked him to tell me what he knew about our family in my youth.

I only remembered the good things. He had a photographic memory and remembered events vividly. It was Nonoy Boloy who confirmed the size of the family farm and provided information about my father's award for the highest rice production in the Iloilo province. He even made a sketch of our family tree. By then, my mother was in a nursing home, unable to speak following a stroke before her ninetieth birthday. Kuya Tito and Ate Vernie had already passed away before I had the chance to sit down and write this memoir. No one I asked was willing to tell me what had happened. My uncle knew the story but he wouldn't tell me about my father's indiscretion. My cousin was my only chance of finding out what happened – why we left our place in Madong and why we migrated to Manila. This story wouldn't make sense if I didn't include it.

According to Nonoy Boloy, Tatay bought a sari-sari store in town and later on moved the business to Lambunao, several towns from Madong. By this time, Tatay had given up farming and concentrated on establishing this business. Tatay went to Lambunao every Wednesday and Saturday. He stocked dry goods and snack foods, which he sold at a lower price so a lot of customers went to his store. Because of the distance involved in going back and forth to Lambunao every Wednesday and Saturday, Tatay bought a permanent place for the convenience store. It allowed him and Kuya Tito to stay there seven days a week and operate the business every day. He also hired a female assistant named Lourdes. Their affair started because they saw each other every day. Nonoy Boloy said that Tatay and Lourdes eloped, leaving my eldest brother to manage the store. Kuya Tito ran away after he was left behind in Lambunao. Later on, the business was sold and closed.

Tatay and Lourdes went to Mindanao, the southern part of the Philippines, where Tatay's eldest brother lived. They stayed there but Tay Hugo, my uncle, did not approve of my father's misdeeds. He contacted his other brothers and sisters and told them about the situation. They unanimously agreed to admonish Tatay and worked together to bring him back to us, his family. Tatay was sent ahead to the northern part of the Philippines in Quezon City where my other uncle lived and was instructed to wait there for us. Tatay's family gathered us together and booked a passage for us to migrate and settle in Quezon City, a suburb of Manila.

Tatay's affair made sense. I remembered Nanay telling us of an incident which made her cry and tremble in front of us. It was very unusual because Nanay never complained or displayed her emotions. The event occurred on one of her trips to Lambunao, several months after our business was established. Nanay told us she almost lost her life. She said that while she was minding the store in the open market, she was chased with a hacking knife by a man she didn't know. She managed to hide under the stalls of some of her friends and later made her escape after making sure that the man was not following her. She prayed hard for her safety. She ran to the main street and took a bus to come back home. When she arrived home alone, she was shaking and very nervous. She must have been in a state of shock because she told us about what happened. She embraced all of us in tears. This was the first time I had seen Nanay crying and vulnerable. Kuya Tito and Ate Vernie weren't at home so I took over as the eldest looking after my younger brothers and sister.

Nanay must have known about the affair but suffered in silence. She never went back to the store. I was too young to understand these things. My poor brother Kuya Tito must have seen and known it all. In the years that followed, he never talked about it.

We were all huddled on a pier in Iloilo City waiting for our ship bound for Manila. It was a long wait because the ship did not arrive until the evening. I didn't know where we were going but I was comforted by the fact that I was with my family. When it arrived, all I could see was the black hull of a huge, tall ship. I shivered in fear and in awe. Nanay asked if I would like a meal. I was hungry so I said yes. She ordered pancit molo, an Iloilo soup delicacy, for us all. The delicious hot soup settled my nerves and stopped my shivering. My feeling of fright might have been due to the sight of a big ship that moored so close to where we were, or it might have been due to awe seeing such a big transport for the first time in my life. It would carry us to an unknown place with an unknown future.

After a long voyage, we arrived at our destination in Murphy, Quezon City. We were taken to a place where we were welcomed by a man introduced to us as our uncle, Tay Luis (my father's younger brother), and his wife, Auntie Ester. Tatay stayed at my uncle's place until we arrived. I don't remember much about our stay with Tay Luis. He was an ex-soldier who fought during World War II and was given accommodation near the army compound where he worked as a civilian. All I could remember was how cramped our room was. It must have been a two-bedroom house because we all stayed in one room.

The transition from a broken family to reconciliation was difficult, especially in a new environment. We struggled against poverty, were berated by a condescending neighbour, and the onus fell on me to help Nanay with household chores. Tatay used his skill as a carpenter to earn a livelihood when we arrived in Quezon City after migrating from Iloilo. We moved from my uncle's place and rented a house in Project 4, Quezon City. Kuya Tito, Ate Vernie and I started school again.

I was thirteen when I started first year high school. Kuya Tito worked at a convenience store owned by the Munoz family at the corner of our street. Later, he got a job as a taxi driver and studied computing at night. He then became the personal driver for Mr Mercado and Mr Brinas, top executives at the Central Bank of the Philippines. On the recommendation of his boss, Kuya Tito started working at the Central Bank. He started at the bottom of the ladder and worked his way up. Because of his hard work and resilience, he was invited to work with the electronic data processing department, forming its data system. He later finished college and became a systems analyst in that department.

Ate Vernie worked in Cubao, Quezon City, as a food assistant to the owner of the house we rented. I never went to the landlord's shop, nor did I see the owner in all the years we rented the house. It was only a few suburbs away, but I had no money to spend on travel. I missed my sister, but I had no choice. I was also busy with household work helping Nanay. Ate Vernie studied commerce while working until she graduated from college.

During this difficult transition in our life, I noticed that Kuya Tito and Ate Vernie walked past by my father without greeting or acknowledging his presence. I thought it odd, but I continued to greet my father every day, whether I was going out or coming into the house. My father or mother did not say anything, but I could sense that there was something wrong. It was only when I was married and old enough to understand that I realised how much my eldest brother and my older sister must have suffered due to our father's indiscretion. Kuya Tito loved my mother very much. He was the apple of my mother's eye. By the same token we, his younger sisters and brothers, loved Kuya Tito. He stood in as a father figure when some of my siblings turned against my father. I accepted my father as he was. It must have been my innocence in not understanding what happened that gave me a non-biased attitude.

My father was a harsh disciplinarian. My younger brother next to me suffered so much because of his vagabond-like ways and defiant attitude. He was valedictorian in his class, intelligent and ambitious but he was rebellious and often clashed with Tatay. I couldn't do anything to shield him from punishment, but I made it a point of being there to support him. Once, my brother got entangled with mischief – it wasn't really a big deal but he got into trouble and went to jail. I was working with the Department of Agrarian Counsel, so I sought the help of my two senior lawyer bosses to get him out of jail. The discipline during our time was strict and harsh.

I never felt the brunt of Tatay's disciplinary anger because I always obeyed him. In fact, it was only from Nanay that I got a painful pinch when I was naughty one time. With Tatay, I never answered back. I always reasoned with him. It was only later that I learnt he didn't punish me because I argued with him, rather than defying him. He told me this once when I was crying due to work problems in my teenage years. He listened to me when I was having a tantrum. This was what Tatay wanted from his children – to talk to him about the problem so he could understand, instead of offering rebellion and defiance. My siblings were jealous of me because they thought I was my father's pet. They didn't know that I also disagreed with him but in a diplomatic way. My brothers and sisters were different. They said nothing but did what they wanted to do. I guess being a teenager is a difficult age for anyone.

We were struggling financially but my father did not want us to owe anything to the convenience store. He wanted us to live within our means and not accumulate debts. This was difficult when income was meagre – only enough for subsistence. I learned financial discipline from my father and it helped me in my financial undertakings when I was older. I became the best budgeter in the family. I could make both ends meet despite hardship and could even save for emergencies.

One time, we were lambasted and called patay-gutom which literally meant 'starved-to-death people' by Nene, one of our neighbours. Her son cried after a quarrel with my brother Eddie, then about four years old. The boys had been playing outside the house. We only knew about the incident when Nene entered our gate in arrogant haste and in a loud and angry voice, berated my mother. My mother was a very peaceful person and would not pick a fight. It was her nature to maintain her dignity and she wouldn't stoop to such a display of emotion in public. She asked what happened. I don't know what Nene said, but Nanay assured her that it would never happen again. She admonished my younger brother, but I knew that she silently cried after this incident because she was deeply hurt by the cruel words.

This episode had a profound effect on me. I was determined to move on. It was a difficult journey.

Chapter 12

Kuya Tito and Ate Vernie had jobs so I stayed home and helped Nanay with the household chores. I helped her clean the house and cook. I laundered, ironed and ran errands. My weekends were all work. No water went through the metered pipes during the day, so I made sure the big water drum Tatay provided was full every day. I connected a long hose from the tap to the drum and let it run during the late evening when the water gushed in full volume. I didn't sleep until this was done. Because of the limited water supply, when I woke at 6 am, I filled the laundry tubs with water and soaked the clothes while there was still water running in the tap. I also filled big plastic containers so we could clean ourselves, water the plants, and wash the dishes. I set aside drinking water in a big jar and used the water from the drum to rinse the laundry, shower, wash the dishes and clean the house. I made sure there was enough water for our needs and no wastage. I allotted a time to give my younger brothers and sister a daily wash. They formed a line from the oldest to the youngest. I scooped the water from the drum to a pail, big enough to wash them all. There was only one towel, one bar of soap and a face washer. The first one to be washed was Fred. I poured water on his head, used the soap from head to foot to cleanse him, scrubbed him with the face towel, rinsed, patted him dry with the towel, and let him go to dress himself. The same process continued with Cora, Ben and Eddie until all of them were clean. Poor Eddie – by the time the towel reached him, it was soggy and damp.

There were eight children in the family by this time. Benjamin, the seventh, was the youngest when we migrated from Iloilo province to Quezon City. Eddie was born when we were in Project 4, Quezon City. Nanay almost died giving birth to Eddie. He was born prematurely. Nanay bled and was rushed to the hospital. I remember visiting Eddie at the hospital. He was in an incubator and had tubes all over his body. We thought he wouldn't survive. When Eddie was brought home, Nanay was still very weak so the bulk of the household chores were placed on me. I did all the laundry, ironing, cooking, cleaning and running of errands. There was no washing machine then and because of the size of our family, every day I was saddled with big tubs of laundry and pans to clean after cooking. My younger brother Francisco was two years younger than me and not much help. Later on, he worked for someone else, which helped when finances became tough.

Looking after my younger siblings and doing all the household chores was very difficult, a heavy task for me. I was sad because we three elder siblings, who were once very close, were separated by poverty and had to work in different places. Kuya Tito, the eldest, stayed in our neighbour's house minding the convenience store. Ate Vernie stayed in Cubao, Quezon City, as a helper for our landlady. Frank, the brother next to me, was in another household helping with chores but he came home at night.

In our culture, the elder siblings look after the younger ones so there was really no choice. Tatay was very tired when he came home from his hard work as a carpenter. When Nanay was strong enough, she did the household duties with my constant help. Finances were tight so I was called to assist a matronly lady in her vanities – I sorted her wardrobe, shoes, facial routine and did little things when she needed assistance. Her husband was much older than her, so all her whims and caprices were provided for. I earned extra money from this to help my family buy food.

When I had free time, my favourite pastime was climbing the friendly santol tree in our backyard. I made small indentations on the big trunk to go up and down the tree. I took nibbles, toys, and a little pillow to my sanctuary. There were times when I spent almost the whole day there. It was peaceful. The thick leaves hid me, and if there was ripe fruit within my reach, I ate it. I would only go down for mealtimes when Nanay called.

Our elderly neighbour Aling Maria wanted to earn money even though she was married to a lawyer. They had a nice house and beautiful grown-up children. The youngest daughter, Rosemarie, was capricious and cheeky. She always wore pretty dresses. She befriended me and sometimes told me secrets about her boyfriends that she didn't want her parents to know. I was fascinated by her stories and kept her secrets.

On weekends, Aling Maria would ask me to go to the market with her. She let me carry the big bayong (a tall, matted bag made of dried nipa leaves with a strong handle to hold heavy weights) which carried her purchases from the market. We took the bus to Marikina, a faraway marketplace, where she bought good quality ingredients to make merienda, which she cooked and I would sell in front of our yard.

She bought a kilo each of bananas (the ones that were rectangular at the end), camote, taro, fresh ripe jackfruits, bilo-bilo, freshly grated mature coconut and sugar. She also bought fresh fish and bread. I carried the heavy bags while we shopped. I was frail and little, so the weight was a burden. When she had finished her shopping, we walked to the bus stop to go home. When we reached our place at Project 4, we still had to walk around five blocks to reach her house. The purchases were heavy for a frail girl like me, but this was my only way of earning extra money to help the family and also to have my own pocket money. My afternoons had to be free to mind the stall in front of our rented house.

When Aling Maria finished cooking the banana cue (bananas cooked in oil and brown sugar) and the halo-halo, she brought them to our place and placed the big pots on the long table in front of our house. She provided a measuring cup and a ladle so I could measure the quantity of snack poured into the buyer's container when they bought the merienda in the afternoon during siesta time, between two and four o'clock. We had afternoon snacks because there was a big gap between lunch and dinner.

The contents of the measuring cup depended upon how much the customers were willing to pay. They were regulars who lived in the neighbourhood. When the day's trading had finished, I earned my income according to how much we had sold during the day and how generous Aling Maria was. This helped me with my pocket money for school and sometimes I gave some money to Nanay to add to her market money. It was hard work. I couldn't have a nap even though I was sleepy. I woke up very early for the trip to the market so by the afternoon, I was really tired. I was in my growing years and wanted to sleep during siesta, but I had no choice because I had to attend to the food stall. Aling Maria relied on me.

The snack stall always generated a good income because Aling Maria saw to it that there were variations of merienda every week. Sometimes, the guinatan would be made of grated fresh corn, glutinous rice, brown sugar and coconut cream. On other days, it would be fried mung bean crushed into small pieces and cooked with glutinous rice, sugar and coconut cream. Or the whole package would consist of cubes of sweet potatoes, taro, cooking bananas cut into round or square pieces, bilo-bilo, tapioca, shreds of ripe fresh jackfruit, vanilla, sugar and coconut cream. At other times, we had three or four slices of banana or camote cue pierced on a stick, depending on the size of the banana or the sliced sweet potato.

We also provided the gulaman (gelatine) drink to complement the afternoon snack. The red, green and yellow moulded gelatine was cut into small cubes, placed in a jug of water with ice and syrup made of dark brown sugar. We added cooked tapioca and lemon grass for extra flavour.

Chapter 13

Kuya Tito, Ate Vernie and I took a break from school during some of these tumultuous years. We didn't resume school until we moved to Quezon City in 1960. I graduated from primary school before my tenth birthday and didn't go to school for two years. I was thirteen when I started first year high school and Ate Vernie was fifteen. Ate Vernie and I both went to Quirino High School in Project 3, Quezon City, a few kilometres from our house. At the time, our suburb had no name and the suburbs were named Projects 1 to 7.

We walked to school from Project 4 where we lived. This was also the year I started having periods. I was at school when it happened, and it stained my school uniform. I didn't know what to do. I felt embarrassed because it made a mark on my skirt. I was lucky that the colour of our skirt was maroon. I was shy and self-conscious because I came from the provinces. My classmates were all born and bred in the city. When I was young, knowledge of the birds and the bees was taboo and not discussed in class or casual conversations.

The initial awkwardness disappeared once I concentrated on my studies. Kuya Tito, Ate Vernie and I had been honour students during our primary grades in our provincial school, so I had to prove that I could do well at the new school. This helped me adjust quickly. I made new friends and learned to speak Tagalog, the national language, a requirement for all students. The Philippines has 7,200 islands and each island has its own dialect. Learning the national language was essential to understand one another regardless of which island you came from. Most of our textbooks were written in English so we had to learn and understand English as well.

Where I came from, we spoke the local dialect, Kinaray-a. My family and I had an edge on speaking dialects and the national language because Tatay was very strict with our education and the literature we read. We were not allowed to read comics. Aside from speaking our local dialect, I also learned Ilongo, our city dialect and Tagalog. Tatay had a habit of buying the two magazines weekly – *Hiligaynon*, written in the Ilongo dialect and *Liwayway*, a literary magazine written in Tagalog. I loved reading these magazines after school because they provided good reading and entertaining stories. They had a comics section, short stories, love stories, news, advertisements and lots of trivia. There was also a section about movie stars.

When we had tests in our national language class, the teacher checked my paper first. Most of the time, I got 100%. If it was 98%, she scribbled the correct answers and then let me help her check my classmates' tests. I was honoured, knowing that my classmates spoke Tagalog, yet they couldn't obtain perfect scores. In our biology class, I loved volunteering to stand up in front of the class and explain the flow of blood from the right ventricle to the left ventricle using the teacher's stick to point to the different parts of the human heart drawn or pasted on the blackboard. I was fascinated with the human body and its parts, the veins and arteries, and the bones in the human body. I could explain the difference between the metacarpals and the metatarsals. I had a sharp mind and had the capacity to memorise and retain what I learned from textbooks.

As part of our biology and science experiments we had projects like growing mushrooms in the dark or bean sprouts. The only thing I didn't like was dissecting insects and worms or preserving butterflies. That gave me a squeamish feeling. In literature, I loved the poetry of Robert Browning, Elizabeth Barrett Browning, Don Johnson, Rudyard Kipling, Ralph Waldo Emerson and other writers of the Romantic era, but my favourite was Percy Bysshe Shelley. The beautiful passages from his 'Ode to the West Wind' and 'To a Skylark' are imprinted in my heart. I wasn't keen on Shakespearean poetry as it was hard for me to understand the English bard. Edgar Allan Poe's 'The Raven' was good, but I found it eerie. We used to recite our favourite poems in front of the class. One of my classmate's favourite was 'The Charge of the Light Brigade' and she recited this with action and emotion.

On one occasion, everyone in the class was assigned to perform a drama or a play to convey our concept of a certain piece of literature. I chose Shelley's 'The Indian Serenade'. I dramatised the poem by picking a male classmate to be the suitor and I took the role of the Indian princess. I wore a red blouse with an American Indian headpiece adorned with feathers. My mother made the blouse to go with my feather headpiece. We couldn't make a real bonfire inside the class so I used a kerosene lamp and let my classmates sit around the pretend bonfire in a typical Indian scene around a tepee. I remember singing the whole 'Indian Serenade' while dancing around the boys gathered around the bonfire. I didn't know I had the capacity to be an actress as well as a producer. In music class, I joined the choir and learned to read a few musical notes.

We also had physical education which included calisthenics, volleyball, softball and dancing. I was poor in geometry and physics, but I managed to pass these subjects by concentrating and putting in extra effort. I hated physics because I couldn't understand mechanics, formulas and equations. The teacher was more inclined to speak with the boys rather than us, the struggling ones. I was poor and had no pocket money to buy snacks during recess, but I managed to get good grades. I will never forget one time when I was hungry. I was in the cafeteria with my classmates during recess. I didn't have any money, not even 25 cents to buy a boiled banana, my favourite snack. I surreptitiously watched my classmates buying snacks while I buried my head in a book. I swallowed in silence and tried to concentrate on my reading. I almost cried. I hated to beg or borrow money. I was proud, even then.

My classmates had wrist watches, several changes of school uniforms, shoes and pocket money, but I only had two sets of uniforms – one to wear while the other one was laundered – and one pair of shoes. I will never forget the time we were hit by a typhoon and we were sent home from school. The Philippines has several typhoons a year, especially during the monsoon months of June to August. I had a small umbrella and there was a hole in my shoe. I stuffed it with cardboard cuttings to stop the dirt filtering into my feet. I had no money and it was my birthday. I walked back home in the rain, hungry and despondent. I was drenched because the strong winds turned my umbrella inside out. When I reached home, there was only a bit of rice and a casserole with nothing but soup and a few leaves of vegetables floating in it. The meat or fish and the rest of the vegetables were all gone. I ate my simple meal of rice and soup with tears in my eyes. I didn't understand why we were so poor.

It was my birthday, the most important day of the year for me! From that day, I vowed that I would do everything in my power never to be hungry again after I left school. This thought stayed with me. It prodded me to study and work hard and gave me a strong determination to succeed.

The following day, I cut cardboard to cover the hole in my still wet shoe and went to school. I kept doing this until I asked my parents to buy me a replacement shoe. I didn't care whether they were hand-me-downs or a new pair, so long as I could have shoes to protect my feet while walking to school. Sometimes after school I would go with my best friend Ching to stay at their house near the school. Her father was a lawyer and her mother was a schoolteacher. They also had a piano. I was served refreshments by their housemaid and I was grateful to have a friend like her. She played the piano very well and one time, I was invited to attend one of her piano recitals held at an exclusive girls' school at Gilmore, Quezon City.

After high school, at the age of sixteen, I wanted to have a regular paying job instead of doing heavy household chores and odd jobs to earn money. I took stenography and typing classes at St Francis Vocational School in Quezon City. Most of my high school classmates went to the University of the Philippines, the State University. I wanted to go too, but my father couldn't afford pocket money and bus fares for me so I decided to study in a vocational school. I asked Tatay to pay my tuition for this short course so I could get a job quickly and help the family.

I went to church every Sunday. After church, I taught catechism to young children in the neighbourhood. When they knew I was coming, they gathered around to listen to Bible stories and learn prayers and songs. I also became an active member of the Legion of Mary and after a few years, I worked on adult cases. As a Legionary, we had a lot of functions and responsibilities. Every year, we renewed our vows and I was blessed to be a part of this group as it strengthened me in my struggles through life. I faced many hardships and obstacles, but they did not deter my wish to better my situation. I was determined to finish college and get on in life. I hardly had time to rest, sleep or enjoy my teenage years, but maybe I was destined to live a different kind of life.

Chapter 14

When I received my Diploma in Stenography and Typing at seventeen, I felt ready to look for a job. I had high grades and was a fast typist. I could type 60–70 words per minute and my stenography speed was 120–160 words per minute using the Greg shorthand. I practised every day until I was proficient. When I was confident of my skills, I asked my parents to speak on my behalf to Attorney Abigania, our lawyer neighbour, about possible employment. He was the husband of Aling Maria, the lady who I had helped with her snack business during my high school days. She was impressed with my diligence, honesty and hard work, so I had a good reference, an important part of finding employment.

After my parents talked to Attorney Abigania, I was asked to report to his office in Manila. I was apprehensive at first but determined to get a job. I was given a stenography and typing test which I passed easily. Attorney Abigania had many connections as a lawyer. He recommended me for employment with the Director of the Office of the Agrarian Counsel in Quezon City. I was hired as stenographer there in 1965 when I was almost 18 years old. That was the start of my working career.

The Agrarian Counsel was on the other side of Quezon City from where I lived, so I had to change buses twice to get to work. Everything was uncharted territory for me, so I felt apprehensive and nervous. I was very shy, too, with little exposure to public life. My clothes, handbag and shoes, were limited. I had only a couple of pairs of decent clothes, one pair of high-heeled shoes and one handbag. I asked a friendly neighbour to teach me how to apply a simple make up to make me look a bit professional. I bought my own powder and lipstick out of my first salary. I asked Mom to buy me some material from that first pay, too. She made me clothes that I designed myself. My wardrobe dilemma was solved when I learned that we were required to wear a uniform. I bought two sets of uniforms initially and added more as I could afford them. I gave the rest of my salary to Nanay to help buy food for the family after I had set aside money for my food and fares. I woke early to prepare lunch and snacks before work as the food stores were far away from the office. It would have taken a good half hour out of my lunch time if I had searched for a place to buy lunch. Also, I was on a tight budget, so I had to be careful with money.

When I became permanent in the job, I enrolled at the University of the East in Manila to get a college degree. I didn't like it there, so I transferred to University of Santo Tomas. I enrolled in the journalism course as an evening student. I wanted to study painting in the Arts and Letters Department, but I couldn't afford the tuition fee and materials. In my country, you cannot prosper unless you are a university graduate. Some students who belonged to affluent families were sent to prestigious universities overseas, or in the case of a socialite, to a finishing school in Paris to assure them of a good job when they returned home.

I was assigned to the Special and Appealed Cases Division of the Agrarian Counsel as a stenographer. I used a manual typewriter, with brands like Underwood, Remington and Olympia. I liked using Underwood and Remington typewriters because the fonts were good and they cut well through the stencil paper for printing.

Typing during the 1960s and 1970s took effort. You had to press hard, especially when using carbon paper to make multiple copies of a document. On legal documents, I used five or six carbon papers to produce seven copies. The original was on legal size bond paper and the carbon copies were on onion-skinned paper. I was lucky if I was typing a letter because they only used one carbon paper to produce the original and a copy. Making mistakes in typing was a challenge, especially with several copies. At first I used an eraser. When typewriters were designed to include a slot for correction tape, the original document looked cleaner. The carbon copies still needed a good eraser to correct mistakes.

My bosses dictated letters and letters of appeal for the Court of Appeals and Supreme Court. This was easy as I was a fast stenographer. I typed the draft, submitted it for correction, and typed the final letters of appeal with several pages of a long document after it had been edited. Aside from the chief and the assistant chief of the division, other lawyers who liked the speed and accuracy of my work asked me to type work for them. There were other stenographers but some of them were slack. They took their time and wouldn't be hurried. I was used to multi-tasking, so I finished the job as soon as possible.

The legal documents were long. There was a need for speed and precision in typing because the documents submitted to the Court of Appeals and Supreme Court had deadlines. Most of the briefs were in stencilled form so they could be run on legal bond paper to produce the several copies needed for submission. We also needed copies for the file and furnished copies to the lawyers of the appellee or the appellant. I had to type hard on the keyboard keys to slice well into the stencil paper so as to make a clear print when it was run to produce copies.

When we had a deadline, everybody was on standby, even the driver. When I finished the documents, they were run in several copies and couriered to the Court of Appeals or the Supreme Court. The boss who wrote the appeal signed the stencil paper before the copies were run. I had to personally sort and staple the pages to ensure there were no errors.

The chief and assistant chief of the division always gave me their work because they were happy with my precision and speed in typing. Sometimes I helped edit what they wrote, earning their appreciation. I was a working student and my college studies had helped me with writing and editing. The long sentences and paragraphs on the legal documents had honed my skills in the English language. I also learned a lot about the narratives of an appeal and some Latin legal terminology.

The assistant chief had a lot of court cases to attend to, so he sometimes picked me up from home on the weekends to dictate an appeal for a client. He did this when he had a court hearing in the provinces and had to leave very early the following morning. By the time he came back the next day, the draft of the document would be finished and all he had to do was read, amend or edit and then I'd finalise the document.

The bosses had great faith in my ability to finish documents with no grammatical or typographical errors and with the pages correctly sorted and stapled before they were couriered. It was hard work, but I was happy and proud to have earned their trust. The other lawyers in the division would give me work as well but they knew that the work I did for the two superiors took priority.

My first job as a stenographer was a stepping-stone to more advanced duties. I was able to develop my abilities and juggle different types of work within strict deadlines. I acquired the habit of precision and speed which I applied to my endeavours throughout my life. Working with lawyers had trained me to think in a particular way. I became focused in my thinking and grasped a word or an idea quickly. When I was assigned to research a certain case or assignment in the library, I did it diligently, making sure that I got the correct pages, the author of the source, the exact quotation, and the relevant information that my bosses needed.

Chapter 15

My high school and college years were full of hard work, study, lofty ideals and ambitions. Finishing university was my priority. I took a full load of subjects from 5 pm to 9 pm every day, with physical education on Thursday nights and Saturdays. Our university uniform was a white baby collar blouse with a blue-ribbon tie and a navy blue pleated skirt. Our physical education uniform was white blouse and a black jumper with big white buttons, and black bloomers, with white rubber shoes.

When I finished work at five o'clock in the afternoon, I rushed to university to attend evening classes. I was a working student so most of the time, I was late for my first subject. There were no concessions when it came to time off work. I had to clock off at exactly 5 pm. If I had examinations I left work early but made up for it by coming early the next day or cutting short my lunch break. Sometimes I took holiday leave to deal with important matters. We used a Bundy clock to slot in upon arrival in the morning, slot out on departure and even going to and from lunch. After work I waited for the jeepney, a small twin-bench bus used for transport, to take me to Espana Boulevard outside the university. I then ran from the gate to the main building and up to the first floor where my first subject was located. It was a good five to ten minutes' run – on my tiny little feet and with a heavy bag of school things.

Most of my classmates were affluent full-time students. Attending evening classes was their personal choice. They were co-ed classes so it was a good way for boys and girls to meet. My sole purpose was to finish my degree, so I didn't get involved with anyone. I saw the girls being driven to the front of the main building and picked up in a Mercedes Benz. They had well-manicured hands, beautiful bags, professional hairdos, and always gathered in groups. I was the only one catching my breath when I arrived at our 5 pm class, ripping the door open and sitting at the far end of the classroom near the door. My professor was lenient because he knew I was a working student. Most of the time, I was in my work clothes, not university uniform. I made up for it by getting high grades. There were times when I was so exhausted that even before the class ended, I would be dozing on and off, especially when the lectures were boring. I sat with the boys as I felt awkward because of the off-hand attitude of the girls. There were some, though, who were nice. One of them was Eden who became my best friend at college.

For dinner, I ate sandwiches I had prepared and bought from work. I munched them during the break or between classes. This meant I never really associated or talked with my classmates as I always squeezed meals into my schedules. Most of my subjects were in the new Arts and Letters building behind the main building. By the time we met for other subjects at the Arts and Letters building, I had finished my food. This made me feel better. There were lucky times when I had the chance to chat with other classmates in the ladies' room before class. If I had the chance, I changed into the university uniform before the next subject.

I attended physical education class on Thursday evenings and swimming classes on Saturdays. I tried not to skip classes as it was hard for me to make up for lost time during working days. I couldn't graduate college without passing the physical education subjects, so I made the effort. There were no exceptions when it came to PE uniforms. I took the uniform with me and changed in the ladies' room if I had PE classes during the week, especially calisthenics and other subjects. I hated it when I wore the black bloomers underneath the black overall skirt with a white blouse. My swimming lessons were always on Saturdays. For swimming classes, I wore a one-piece black bathing suit under my PE uniform before I went to class.

Another reason my schedule was tight was because I went to the library on Saturdays after swimming lessons. I could see my other classmates spending time with boyfriends or girlfriends. I tried to avoid a relationship as I wanted to escape my dreadful situation and provide a better future for my family and myself. There was this guy who was a playboy and had a different girlfriend every semester. His name was Ray. Sometimes he chatted with me before class, but I made a point of sitting between two male classmates so Ray couldn't sit beside me. This guy was good-looking and my type, but I couldn't afford to be distracted by a boyfriend. I was probably labelled a snob or stand-offish, but I didn't care. I was friendly and affectionate with the guys who didn't show any interest in me. I was determined to finish college, whatever the cost.

Every day, I woke at around 5.30 am to prepare my lunch and nibbles. I left home early to allow time to get to work. Working and studying full time was taxing. I felt constantly sleep-deprived and it was worse when there was a deluge or a typhoon. This made transport difficult because Espana Boulevard, the street in front of the university where I got out of the jeepney, always flooded.

The rainy season was stressful. I was always soaked before I reached class. The same thing happened when I went home. While my female classmates were chauffeur-driven, immaculate in their uniforms, I looked like a wet chicken and had to dry myself in the ladies' room before I went into class.

I braved crossing the flooded street to get home quicker, but my shoes were soaked in filthy drain water. I had to stand in the bus all the way to Cubao, a suburb near home, because the bus was full of passengers coming from Quiapo – the station where most people got off – but they were replaced by passengers returning home. I was already exhausted from work and study, but I had no choice. If I got a seat, I was lucky. It gave me a chance to close my eyes and rest on the long journey home.

There was another route to avoid the flooded road in front of the university. It was at the back of the university at Dapitan Street. This was circuitous and it added an hour to my travel time. I had to go to Quiapo, the main station, where I could get direct transport and a seat to go home. I only took this route if I didn't want my shoes to get soaked or if I wanted to be sure of a seat on the bus. Otherwise, I braved it and crossed the flooded street at Espana Boulevard. There were no overpass bridges. The putrid water sometimes reached up to my knees. This was an unpleasant road to travel, well known to the public, especially in light or heavy rain.

The rain and floods were a menace because they ruined my shoes and uniform. I had to iron my changeover clothes as soon as I got home and dry my shoes by whatever means. Before going home, I bought hot food from the stalls outside the university to eat dinner while I waited for the bus home. It was always a long wait. I finished classes every night at 9 pm, and by the time I reached home, it was already 10 or 11 pm if I was lucky. It could be after midnight if there was a typhoon. When I reached home, I was still hungry, so I ate a late dinner if there was any food left. I was exhausted, but I had to do my assignments, prepare my things for work the following day, and get up at five or six o'clock in the morning to cook my lunch and prepare my sandwiches. Sometimes I didn't sleep until 1 am despite the fact that I had to wake up early the following day. By the time I got to work, I was already exhausted and if I could close my eyes during the bus trip, I counted that as a blessing.

When I was at work, I forgot everything because it was so busy. I was always engrossed in whatever I did. I had to concentrate because I couldn't fail the bosses who had entrusted me with their work. The good thing about taking lunch and heating it up in the office was that it gave me time to take a nap even just for 20 minutes during my one-hour lunch break. This re-energised me to resume work and study at night.

Looking back, I can't believe how I managed to handle an exacting job and study full time at night. It was probably because I had a dream – to improve my lot and that of my family. This gave me the determination to succeed and not to be diverted by hardship, difficulty or hindrance. This dream drove me to persist despite the many times that I was tempted to give in. It was really tough but I soldiered on, although sometimes I wondered if it was really worth it. I was getting good grades and I wanted to apply for a scholarship so my tuition fee would be free, but I had no time to associate with others who had scholarship grants. I was working and had no time to study in the library or socialise with classmates afterwards. My time was so limited I couldn't even stay back for a short chat with classmates.

When I wanted to give up, I felt as if one foot was in the grave and the other foot was pulling me wearily, just enough to keep going and prevent me from sinking.

I didn't finish my degree in one term because I needed to finish some subjects. The subjects I needed to graduate were offered in summer classes. In the summer of 1970, I graduated with a Bachelor of Literature in Journalism degree from the University of Santo Tomas. It took me four years and one summer to finish the course. It was difficult and challenging but I made it. I didn't attend my graduation ceremony. I had a graduation picture taken, ordered my college ring and paid for my intricately designed degree all written in Latin.

When I finished university, I felt a deep sense of release. A heavy burden had been lifted from my chest. One of my professors advised me not to give up my job as a stenographic reporter at the Department of Justice as I was already there, earning an income, while my classmates were still struggling and finding it hard to get a job. I could see the wisdom of his advice. It would have been risky to give up a guaranteed income. I couldn't leave my family hungry just to pursue my own ambitions. Writing wouldn't have provided me with an income until I got a placement or had a by-line story published.

My friendship with Eden developed during our college days. Her dad was a lawyer and her mom a beautiful socialite housewife. They lived in a two-storey house in Santa Mesa, Manila. Eden was caring, kind and sincere and had no conceit in her attitude towards me. She became my best friend. She is beautiful and tall for a Filipina, very charming, with dimples when she smiles. She had several suitors. I was a working student, so we had our girly talks during weekends. I usually went to their place and she fed me delicious food. She was a good cook. At other times, she would come to our house at Project 4 and cook for us. I have to admit I wasn't much of a cook.

Eden stopped going to university when her dad passed away. I don't know the full story, but it seemed that her father, a well-known lawyer, didn't leave anything to them despite being affluent and having hectares of land and properties in the northern Philippines (Ilocos Norte). The properties were taken over by her dad's siblings and relatives, depriving Eden and her siblings of what was rightfully theirs. It was sad because her father did not leave a will and they had no means of fighting for what belonged to them as heirs. They became poor and the onus of providing bread and butter for the family fell on Eden.

Eden and I are still close friends. We had our share of joys and sorrows and even after all those years, having gone through the difficult years of our lives – failed marriages, grown-up children, and deaths in our families – we are still kindred spirits.

Chapter 16

When I started working, I gave most of my pay to my mother to help with food and other necessities. I always lived on a strict budget. I hardly bought any new dresses, shoes or bags – only the bare necessities to make me look professional at work. I couldn't even afford vitamin supplements. I welcomed handouts, especially clothes, to save money. Nanay never asked me for money but she knew that I willingly contributed to the family expenses. Deep in my heart, I knew what it meant to be hungry. I couldn't enjoy the good things if I knew that my family was doing without.

On weekends, I still helped Nanay with housework, going to the market, cooking and strictly apportioning the food on younger siblings' plates. It was always Nanay and I who missed out. If one of my brothers complained, I admonished him firmly. My younger sister was more considerate and took whatever was apportioned to her. Nanay was always lenient and sometimes my younger brothers took advantage, hiding meat or fish under the rice and asking for more. When one of my brothers was caught, it made me stricter and I took no notice when they next cried wolf.

Sometimes I cried because I earned the money, I did the budgeting and marketing, I cooked and apportioned the food, yet I was the one who always missed out. Nanay was also deprived of good food to sustain her while doing all the housework, looking after the needs of my father and my younger siblings. I thought of a better way to give Nanay her sustenance, away from the prying eyes of my siblings. At night after I came home from the university, I would place a bag of good pastries or food for her breakfast near her pillow so when she woke, she would see the food when she made the bed in the morning. She always thanked me in the morning before I went to work. I also made sure she took a fair portion of food herself before she apportioned it to my always hungry younger siblings.

When I was working at the Department of Justice, I sent Nanay to St Francis Vocational School where I finished my steno-typing course. She wanted to study dressmaking which she loved to do, so I paid her tuition. When she finished the course, she was qualified to accept sewing jobs from neighbours and friends. This allowed her to make a living without leaving the house and it helped with finances. Nanay did everything to perfection. She was good at fitting and measurement. She tailor-made all my clothes apart from my uniforms. I bought the material and designed my clothes while she cut, measured and sewed them expertly. She started taking orders from customers in the neighbourhood on top of her busy schedule as a housewife. I made a point of doing most of the chores on weekends to help her. Nanay made my gown when I had my first formal dinner at work. I was the only stenographer invited to the occasion and was seated in the midst of my lawyer bosses.

Before I graduated, while busy with studies and work, I became interested in writing. When one of my officemates resigned from work and started a publishing company, I became a regular contributor to his magazine. It was a movie magazine called *Virgo* (Magazine of the Stars). I attended the publisher's social gatherings and noted how Dindo, the publisher, interacted with movie stars. I had read the first edition of the magazine and decided I could be a feature writer. I asked Dindo to help me get an identification card with the magazine logo so I could start interviewing movie stars. He was impressed by my determination and knew how dedicated I was. His wife Anita and I were work mates.

My wish was granted. I got the identification card as a contributing writer to *Virgo Movie Magazine*. I wanted to prove that I could do it, so I squeezed interviews with movie stars into the weekends, late nights or after location shoots. Each month, I was given a new assignment and a deadline.

My first assignment was with a budding starlet new to the movie world. I was full of nerves. I summarised my questions and read them thoroughly before the interview. My accreditation as a *Virgo Movie Magazine* writer gave me confidence. The starlet was very nice and cooperative, and the interview went well. I made several drafts before I submitted the finished article directly to the publisher. I was apprehensive about whether it would be approved. Dindo had a very pleasant editor whom I met at the magazine's social gatherings. Meanwhile, I had my job as a backup in case writing didn't provide an income.

When the magazine came out, I was surprised to see my by-line, my very own name, printed as author of the article, and although the words and presentation were amateurish, there it was staring at me – my very own first movie article with pictures of the starlet taken by the magazine's photographers. I was thrilled that my dream of becoming a writer had come true. It was an auspicious beginning for me. I was thrilled, too, when I was given my first payment as a writer. Despite my hectic schedule at work and school, I accepted other interview assignments.

It was good while it lasted. During my last years in university, though, my schedule became extremely tight. The assistant chief of my department, who lived nearby, asked me to work on Sundays sometimes. He dictated the briefs he wanted submitted on a particular case before he flew to another island to attend a court hearing. I also had to finish my thesis, without which I could not graduate from university. I had no choice but to give up my sideline as a writer, which had also been a good source of additional income for me and my family. It just wasn't possible to fit interviews into my already overloaded schedule.

I finally got my university degree in the summer of 1970. It was a relief not to have to rush to university after work. It also gave me time to get to sleep earlier and to catch up with my personal life. I could go out on dates, chaperoned by my elder sister. In those days, you couldn't go out on a date without a chaperone. It was fun, though, just to feel what it was like to be a lady.

Work was challenging. I was promoted to stenographic reporter when my former boss at the Agrarian Counsel recommended me to the Department of Justice. It was hard work but with minimal pay, so I decided to take a postgraduate course to improve myself and escape my very taxing job. I enrolled at the University of the East for a Master of Public Administration. In my second year I met my first real boyfriend, who later became my husband.

My elderly colleague Tio Pascual at the Department of Justice introduced me to Tomas. Tio Pascual used to chat with me during office breaks. He'd say hi or wave to me whenever he was around. I didn't know he had a nephew until he introduced Tommy to me. Tommy's father had a pest control business, but Tommy had opted to be independent. He had a job of his own, only working for the family business on weekends. Tomas was very keen and pursued me daily. He was a chain smoker and a drinker. I told him I do not date men who smoke and drink. I was surprised when he totally stopped smoking a week after we dated, and he also cut down on his drinking. He was always waiting for me after I finished work. He was a bailiff at a local court and finished work earlier than me. He was sincere and intelligent, so I gave him the benefit of the doubt. He would ring me every day just to hear my voice and to have a chat before he saw me in the evening. He escorted me home daily, stayed until late at night just to be with me and then went home, more than an hour's trip at that hour. There were only a few buses so he had to walk quite a way from the bus stop to his home. The weekends were also full of him. I was hooked without even knowing it. I did not want to date during my college days because I wanted to finish college. Now that I had finished college, I thought it was time to have a boyfriend.

Chapter 17

After three months of courtship, Tomas asked his parents to arrange a meeting with my parents to ask for my hand in marriage. We called it pamanhikan, this tradition of a man's parents asking permission from the woman's parents for her hand in marriage. The woman's parents have to agree to relinquish their daughter. If the woman's parents don't agree with the daughter's choice, they can refuse. This sometimes resulted in the couple eloping.

Mine agreed so, there I was, married at the age of twenty-five. It was a simple, no-fuss wedding. We spent our own money on the wedding and bought only the necessities to build a new life away from our parents, rather than splurging on a lavish wedding and burying ourselves in debt before we even started life together.

I bought the material for my wedding dress and those of the bridesmaids. Mom made my wedding gown that I designed myself. It was simple, with clusters of beads on the front bodice as the only ornament. A neighbour helped me put my makeup on during my wedding day. I didn't like the makeup because it was so thick. I looked like a different person. My husband was twenty-six and I was twenty-five when we got married. After the wedding, we moved to a small rented flat a few blocks from my parent's place.

One week after our church wedding, my husband's true colours started to emerge. That Sunday, I prepared to go to church as usual but Tomas insisted we go to his church, Iglesia ni Cristo, the Church of Christ. I was surprised because we were married in a Catholic church. He was born and baptised a Catholic and this appeared on his baptismal record. It was the reason we only had to wait one month to comply with the church's marriage ban rules.

Despite my surprise and initial shock, I agreed, as a dutiful wife. I was a staunch Catholic but going to his church would not undermine my belief. It would make him happy if I went with him. He didn't stop me going to the Catholic church, so I thought it was fair to be open-minded. What I didn't know was that my husband's whole family had converted to the Iglesia ni Kristo belief. This had been kept from me.

Our first few months were a novelty in other ways. I didn't know anything about married life, what to expect, or what the future held. I was naïve and innocent, but I wanted to have a family of my own. I took on the challenge and plunged in without hesitation. I was very independent before I got married. I'd made a decision and I would stick to it. I believed that my husband would always be there to love, support and be with me throughout my life. In addition, I had a duty to my own family.

I became pregnant straight away. I didn't expect it to be that quick, but there I was, adjusting to a different kind of life, with a husband and a bunch of in-laws and pregnant too. Even when I was three months pregnant, my stomach was still flat. I still wore my short skirt, with my hair in pigtails and ran around in rubber shoes. Some people thought I was a teenager with her boyfriend.

We moved from the small rented granny flat near my parents' place, to Eden's place at Santa Mesa, near my obstetrician-gynaecologist. Doctor Mendiola was one of the best, so I decided to let her monitor my pregnancy. Tomas continued his college studies at night. He was brilliant in his own way and knew a lot of things – another jack of all trades. He had been a policeman before he got the job as court bailiff. He had a knack for fixing cars, so he was studying mechanical engineering. It was difficult for both of us, juggling work and family, but we had to do this to prosper and make a better future for our child. We were both working so we were able to manage our expenses. Even so, we lived on a tight budget.

Our place was small, with a smell of sewage emanating from somewhere, so it was unhealthy. My pregnancy was difficult. I might have had a miscarriage had it not been for my brilliant lady doctor who gave me tablets to help my foetus cling. She let me rest from work for one month. I filed an application for leave of absence. I was under a lot of stress at this time. I had been transferred to a department on the third floor with new bosses. There had been a change of administration in my old department and the new head brought in new staff. There were no lifts to the third floor, so I had to walk up and down the stairs several times during the day taking documents from one department to another.

There was much to adapt to – a change of work roles, becoming pregnant, adjusting to married life, giving financial assistance to both my family and my in-laws, discovering my husband's skeletons in the closet and his resumption of drinking. I wasn't prepared for such sudden and dramatic changes. I was thankful that he totally stopped smoking. That probably saved his life in later years.

I was unhappy with my new bosses and the new work, which provided neither challenge nor motivation. From being a stenographic reporter doing challenging work under two undersecretaries of justice to working at a boring typing job, running errands for three or four lawyers wasn't my idea of work satisfaction. I was unhappy but I couldn't give up work because I was carrying a child who needed all the financial support I could provide.

My mother-in-law and members of my husband's family assisted me in household chores. Mamang, my husband's mother, was a sweet and a caring mother-in-law. Tomas was very close to her and I warmed to her due to her motherly love and affection. She was very cuddly and always had a ready smile.

When I gave birth to my son Davis in 1973, we went back to my parents' place in Quezon City. Davis was a source of joy to our family. He was the first grandchild so my parents, brothers and sisters, spoilt him, especially Ate Vernie. My parents looked after him when I went back to work a month after I gave birth. I was only allowed one month's maternity leave. I breastfed Davis for seven months until my milk dried up. He had baby formula while I was at work. I had looked after my younger brothers and sister but having my own baby was a new experience. I kept a diary of his first words, first steps, first haircut – all his 'firsts'. All my tiredness and stress disappeared when I came home, and he ran to welcome me with a cuddle and kisses.

Tatay built him a crib. When he was able to stand, Tatay made him a big playpen, a potty and a walking support we called an andador. It had a round hole on top where Davis could get in, with support for his upper body. The wide circular base allowed him to walk freely without tripping. Tatay could do almost any kind of carpentry from building a house and furniture to ordinary household things.

Tatay was very organised. He kept his carpentry tools in a big box when he travelled to build furniture or to do handyman jobs. There was a time when his entire toolbox was stolen. The money spent on those tools was sufficient to feed us for a few months but the heartless cheat, as most thieves are, didn't care. It was hard for us without my father's carpentry tools. They were expensive and Tatay had accumulated them through hard work. We survived hand to mouth until he slowly bought his tools one at a time and was able to work again. Nanay supplemented Tatay's income by taking in sewing jobs from friends in the neighbourhood after she finished her vocational course.

Chapter 18

My job as a stenographic reporter enabled me to get a mortgage on a housing project being built at Sampaguita Village, San Pedro, Laguna. It was faraway, in a new subdivision and entailed several changes of transport, but I needed a house for my child and a place to call my own. Also, being on the outskirts of Manila, away from the hustle and bustle and congested traffic, it was quiet and unpolluted.

When our house was finished, I took some leave and we moved in straight away. We were among the early occupants in the village. The houses on the neighbouring lots were still being built. There was one neighbour in front of our house, a couple with a young daughter, and another to the right. At night, it could be scary because there were no streetlights and the whole place was dark and lonely.

I was scared especially at night when I heard the *tik tik* sounds of a flying bat – or was it a witch in the form of a night creature that flew around the house? Once, a creature landed with a loud thud on our roof. My son was crying non-stop at that time, so I held him close to my breast and never put him down. If I switched off the lights, the noise circling the house became louder and sometimes came very close to the windows of the room where we were huddled. I held my Holy Rosary and prayed until the commotion stopped. Then my son and I slept, exhausted.

Sometimes my husband came home late at night. There was no jeepney service so late in the evening, so he would walk home from town.

When we moved, we were on a very strict budget. My mortgage repayments were automatically deducted from my salary. Transport was expensive and my husband was on a minimum wage and was studying part-time. It was also our custom to help immediate relatives who needed financial assistance. It was hard to believe when blessings came our way. There was an ampalaya or bitter gourd growing on the side of the house which never stopped bearing fruit. I cooked a lot of different dishes with it. I cooked it with eggs and tomatoes in the morning, added it to boiled green mung beans with slices of pork or chicken, sautéd it with beef, and made many other dishes out of this one vegetable. It helped tide us over until we recovered from the initial moving expenses.

I couldn't give up work, so I needed someone to look after Davis. My mother-in-law looked for a housemaid from the provinces to be a live-in nanny while I was at work. I looked after him on weekends while the housemaid assisted me with household work. I used to post feeding and other instructions on the fridge. It tore my heart to leave Davis with a housemaid who was young and knew little about childcare, but I had no choice. Either I worked or we starved. My husband couldn't repay the mortgage while he was studying. It was up to me.

It took over an hour to travel to work. I took a jeepney to town, a bus to the terminal, and another jeepney to work. It took a lot longer to get home if I shopped for food at the markets. If I missed the scheduled time of the jeepney to my subdivision, I took a tricycle, a motorised three-wheeled vehicle. This was okay on ordinary days but if it rained, it was doubly hard due to traffic congestion. If I reached town late, there were only a few jeepneys travelling to our village. It was a blessing when tricycles came along, because they provided transport when the jeepneys finished at night. Some of the tricycle drivers refused to take us when it was really dark because there were risks on the unlit, hilly and uninhabited parts on the way to the village.

I convinced my eldest brother who was working at the Central Bank of the Philippines to buy a property near us. He chose a lot at the end of our street, which was convenient. When his purchase was settled and the house was finished, Nanay, Tatay and the rest of the family moved to Sampaguita Village. It was a blessing because my mother, father, brothers and sisters were there to help me look after my son. Nanay and Tatay would always look after him, even though they lived in my eldest brother's house. This made me breathe easier about my son while I was working. My job was demanding and stressful enough.

When my housemaid wanted to go home because she was homesick, we let her go with all travel expenses paid and I left Davis in my parents' care. After work I would stop at the markets to buy food and groceries. Then I would pick up Davis from my brother's house, cook dinner, wash up, do the housework and prepare his things for the following morning as well as my working clothes and my husband's. It was exhausting but I was determined to have my own house, a good job and make a better future for my son. He made me strong despite the difficulties. It was always a joy to see Davis when I came home after an exhausting day at work and the long travel. We enjoyed the time we spent together, a quality time of loving and caring. I loved it when he acted like a little man, dressing himself up, watching what I did and trying to help in the kitchen. He devoured food. He especially loved green mussel soup cooked with ginger and fresh chilli leaves.

I taught Davis at an early age to love reading books. He was easy to teach and learned quickly, only asking questions when something was complicated. I was proud of his inquisitive mind and ability to figure things out. It was a joy seeing him so independent at a young age. He was a colicky baby but when he moved to solid food, that stopped.

We struggled but we survived. There were times I had to take my son to the office if there was no one to look after him. We had a private room at work and my lawyer bosses looked after him while I worked. I took all his things with me – thermos, milk bottles, extra clothes, food, his favourite toy and book. It was especially hard to run after buses and jeepneys with a big bag full of his things and with a child in my arms wearing high heels and work clothes. By the time I retired to bed, I was exhausted.

I was young and ambitious and determined to get out of the rut we were in, so I applied for better positions in other offices. I passed a gruelling examination at the Central Bank. Despite having passed two days of tests, I was still asked for a recommendation from my bosses. Getting a job then was very political. You always needed someone in power to recommend you. I was annoyed by this system, so I didn't pursue the position.

It so happened that at the time, my father-in-law and mother in-law told my husband that if I was willing to work overseas, there was an administrative position available with secretarial and typing work rolled into the one position. They knew I had the capabilities of an all-rounder, so they recommended me. The brother of my mother-in-law was a retired diplomat who needed someone to do administrative work while they were setting up an office in Taipei. It was a good opportunity and the salary was better, so I agreed. I knew I was capable and I wasn't scared of uncharted territory if I could improve our lot.

I was interviewed by the director of the Asian Exchange Center at his house in Dasmarinas Village, Makati. I had only been once to this affluent place during my college days when we had our university party at a classmate's house. It was a mansion with a den where you could get lost in a maze of subdued lights. It was also the first time I had ever drunk a real cocktail, and it made me tipsy. The director's house was big, with imported carpets, but the surrounding houses were even more opulent. I could see the gap between the rich and the poor. I was given documents to read and sign for the offer of employment. I knew that if I didn't take this opportunity, I would never leave and pursue my dream of giving my family and myself a better chance in life. I accepted the offer and sealed my fate. I was heading into the unknown, but it did not faze me a bit. I believed that wherever I went, God would always be there to guide and protect me.

I discussed the options with my family. My son and husband would follow in a few months' time after I settled down in Taiwan. But a surprise was in store.

At a family gathering in my brother's house Aunt Natividad, Nanay's elder sister, told me I was pregnant. I asked her how she knew. She said it showed in my eyes. I didn't believe her.

She wasn't a doctor. She had that uncanny ability to know things like my mother, but I didn't believe she could read my eyes. I didn't have any symptoms of being pregnant – not even morning sickness. She said I looked haggard and despite my explanation that I was just tired, she insisted I was pregnant. To satisfy my curiosity and find out whether my aunt was right, I had a check-up. Lo and behold! My aunt was spot on! I was a few weeks' pregnant!

It was indeed amazing that my aunt with no formal education could tell I was pregnant by looking into my eyes. She had lived all her life on the farm and was known for her strong devotion and prayerful life. Was it due to her observations of women in the past and the absence of doctors that she came to know these things? This was the aunt who looked after me when I was young, the one who loved and looked after me as if I was her own child, while Nanay was busy. She was the one who got annoyed when I was supposed to answer her litany of prayers with *Ora pro nobis* or *Amen*, but I got bored and ran outside to play.

My pregnancy posed a dilemma as I had already accepted the foreign job offer. I deliberated as to whether I should take the foreign assignment, keep the baby, or stay in the Philippines. I prayed for guidance. My family was very supportive. In the end, my decision was to keep the baby and the job. What would happen next was up to the Lord. All I knew was that the baby was a blessing. I was determined to take this chance of a lifetime. I was confident that I would be guided along the way. I continued my preparations for my departure for Taiwan.

It tore my heart to leave my two-year-old son, but my Mom, Dad, and my brothers and sisters would look after him. Tomas and Davis were to follow after I had settled down. I would need a live-in nanny to look after my son while I was working full time so my mother-in-law took charge of finding someone from the provinces to be a reliable live-in nanny.

Chapter 19

The director and assistant director of the Asian Exchange Center had gone ahead to establish our office in Taipei. My son Davis, my parents, my brother Fred and my husband sent me off at the airport. While we were waiting for my flight, Davis took my sunglass and posed for a picture. He looked so cute with his cheeky smile. I was sad to leave him, but I knew he was in good hands.

My first overseas travel with Thai International Airways was pleasant. It took off and landed 'smooth as silk', as advertised. The stewardess pinned a beautiful orchid corsage on my blazer before we took off. I was met at Taipei airport by the assistant director and the office driver. It was freezing cold. My thin corduroy jacket wasn't warm enough. Mom made it, like all my clothes, including some maternity gowns and long-sleeved dresses so I didn't have to buy clothes when I arrived.

There was a welcome dinner for me that night. There was food in abundance, but I couldn't manage the chopsticks and I was too shy to ask for a spoon and fork. The Chinese ladies serving food wore long skirts with a high slit on the side, showing their beautiful, shapely legs. The bountiful courses of food placed on the round table went around as everyone helped themselves. Conversation was lively for the entire three-hour dinner.

Our first office location was at Imperial Hotel in Lin Shen Road in the city. The staff all stayed at the hotel. After dinner, I went to my room and placed my beautiful corsage on the bedside table before bed. I was still hungry, but I didn't know where to shop for food. Then I heard a knock on the door. I was surprised when a hotel attendant delivered a plateful of food with fork and spoon and some fruit. The assistant director had been confidentially advised of my pregnancy beforehand. He must have observed that I hadn't eaten much, so he sent the food to my room. I was thirsty but I didn't know how to order water. Waiters and hotel attendants didn't speak English then. I motioned for a bottle of water to drink. The hotel attendant disappeared and when he came back, he gave me a family-sized bottle of lemonade and a glass. The next day, I asked the office driver what 'bottle of water' was in Chinese. He told me it was 'ping shui'. Water wasn't normally served in restaurants. They drank tea instead.

The following day, I familiarised myself with the office work and in the evening, we went shopping. I was given an advance to prepare for winter. It was still cold in February so I bought bed linen, quilts, thicker night gowns and a few winter clothes.

Staying in the hotel was expensive, so after a month or two we moved to a residential area in Tien Mou. The leased office was a big two-storey house owned by a wealthy business family who lived nearby. I was offered accommodation by the director's wife to tide me over. It was a three-bedroom house with a large lounge room. I stayed there while looking for a place to stay. With no heating, it was freezing at night despite the flannelette pyjamas I'd brought from the Philippines and the thin woollen blanket I recently bought. Gee! It was a difficult transition from a tropical country to a winter-weather land.

The director and assistant director leased the whole building apartment near our office to accommodate the staff. The driver, the cleaner and the tea lady were hired locally. They were both bilingual. It helped to be able to tell them what we needed. George, the director's driver, was a native Taiwanese who spoke good English and was a reliable and a knowledgeable man. He was skilled in a lot of things, from the most mundane request to the demands of his job as an overall assistant to all of us. He helped us settle in and become attuned to Taiwanese local ways and customs. He guided us in where to go, where to shop, told us where to find the best restaurants and hotels, important people to see and tourist spots. He helped us look for furniture because we lived in unfurnished apartments. Mine was on the first floor with two bedrooms to accommodate my family and the housemaid who would be joining us. The finance officer and his wife came first, followed by the remaining staff. The three single men occupied the second floor while the finance officer rented a flat nearby.

I encountered a lot of difficulties during this time. I knew no one in Taipei except the people I worked with. There was also the language barrier. Almost no one spoke English then. I was not easily discouraged. Once I set my heart and mind on what I wanted to do, I stood my ground. I needed to survive and survive I did. The baby I was carrying was dependent on me to survive.

It took me a while to find a gynaecologist to monitor my pregnancy. I trusted God to guide me in my chosen path. I found a doctor who worked at the Seventh Day Adventist hospital on the outskirts of the city. It was a long journey to see him once a month. Meanwhile, I managed to find some local friends, especially young people who were willing to practise their English with me while I learned basic conversational Chinese with them. It was a two-way affair that benefited us all.

The assistant director was a workaholic, so I worked beyond eight hours every day. He acquired this trait when working in Japan, according to his wife, who confided in me during one of our social functions. His life was centred on his career and work. It was a very hectic work schedule and I could scarcely get a tea break, much less leave of absence. We were a small office, so we had to work as a team. Luckily, I didn't have a difficult pregnancy this time. All the same, I was exhausted after work.

The three single male staff were young, and they always came home late. Our office was near our apartment so after work, I went straight home. I had virtually no social life outside work. I was always the one to switch on the lights at the stairs when I came home at night.

Before the male staff arrived in Taipei, I was alone in the two-storey building. I was scared because I could hear the sound of furniture being moved upstairs when I knew no one lived there. I learned later on that the owner of the apartment building had died in a motorcycle accident. He was the son of the owner of the building we leased as an office. Shivers!

One time, the security guard buzzed me at night, wanting to come up to check my apartment. I said no as I was ready to sleep. I assured him everything was alright. Afterwards, I had a chain lock installed. I knew he was doing his rounds when I saw his flashlight roaming all over the building at night.

I prayed the Holy Rosary all the time so I didn't feel alone and to make me strong. Sometimes I finished two decades before I fell asleep. I was alone, vulnerable and pregnant. Although I was scared, I'd chosen this undertaking to give my family a better life, so I had to be strong. I wrote in my diary at night and often sent letters to the Philippines. We had no landlines in our apartment and mobile phones didn't exist then. I missed my son and all of my family so much. I read letters from Mom telling me that he missed me. This made me cry even more. Mom said that every time an airplane or helicopter passed by, Davis would look up on the horizon, point up and say 'Mama' thinking that I was on that aircraft. The last time he saw me, he was at the airport saying goodbye. He called helicopter 'heliteytey' in his two-year old baby talk. Oh, how I missed him!

When most of the remaining staff arrived, the office was in full operation and I was busier. The wife of one of my older workmates was friendly so I had someone to talk to. Sometimes she came to my place. I also made friends with the local ladies and things weren't so lonely. They were considerate because I was full of fun despite being pregnant. The wives of our director and assistant director who later on knew about my condition, showed concern. I worked very hard and efficiently so the bosses had no complaints. I was a stenographic reporter in my previous job, so it was easy for me to take down dictation and write correspondence. I also did all the office administration.

After I familiarised myself with my new surroundings, I started to explore on my own. By this time, I had learned a little conversational Chinese. Shopping was always fun. I found the things I needed easily as the local driver told us where to shop. Most of my shopping was for baby things. I got nappies, baby clothes, a cot, bottles. I played safe with colours. I didn't know whether I could find out the baby's sex but even if I could have, I didn't want to know. I always wanted to accept my child whether a boy or a girl. Actually, I thought it was another boy the way the baby kicked and moved inside my womb. Before my family came, I wasn't careful with the food I ate. I would drink a family-sized Pepsi while watching TV. I indulged in salty dried watermelon seeds which were big and easy to crack open. I ate yummy Chinese delicacies. I didn't realise that I was courting trouble by eating the big 'no-no' stuff for a pregnant woman. If, at the back of my mind I suspected it was bad for me, I didn't care. I was lonely and had no one to talk to. I was going up and down to and from my apartment every day, sometimes with heavy groceries. Despite this, I was extra careful not to slip as no one was there to help me in case of an emergency.

After three months, Tommy and Davis arrived. A live-in nanny as well as housekeeper, came with them. By this time, my son was two years and nine months old. He was already speaking fluently. He was a source of joy – cheeky, active and into everything. It was a time of adjustment for all of them in a foreign country where very few people spoke English. While I was busy in the office, my husband and the live-in housekeeper looked after my son and did the household work. I was already six months pregnant and had difficulty running around. My stomach was huge. One of my single male officemates thought I was ready to give birth because of my size. I asked my doctor if I had to diet. I was told no, so I did not control my food intake.

One occurrence gave me a fright and almost knocked the life out of me. Davis had placed a carton on the balcony. He climbed on top of it and was looking down when I came home from shopping. I saw him waving at me when I looked up. I ran up the stairs and grabbed him, screaming in horror. I was furious with the nanny and my husband who had not been vigilant. I cautioned Davis that he should never do that again, telling him he would die if he fell to the ground. He understood and it never happened again. We made sure that there were only heavy chairs to sit on, no stools, no boxes of any kind to stand on, and the balcony was locked at all times to prevent any future untoward incidents.

The nanny loved going around the Tien Mou area and sometimes brought my son to visit the assistant director's wife, who I called Mommy. She was fond of my son. During one of these visits in summertime my son became seriously ill and it developed into bronco-pneumonia. I learned afterwards what happened. Davis was perspiring profusely after he woke up from his afternoon nap. They exposed his back directly to the high-speed electric fan to make him feel cooler. The minders did not realise that this would be bad for a child wet with perspiration. I was furious because Davis was prone to colds and had a low resistance. The nanny could have wiped off his sweat first and let him drink water before exposing his back to the fan.

This was a tough time for me. Our office was nearby so I went home to attend to my son at lunch time. He had high fevers at night and his cough was incessant, so we took him to the doctor. His cough continued for days. I rocked him every night in my arms until he slept. I was tired from work and by the time I went to bed, I was exhausted. I had to get up around three times during the night to monitor him every time he coughed. I made sure his back was not wet with sweat. This vigil went on for a few days. I was also nearing the birth of my second child.

Two weeks before my second baby was due, my waters broke while I was holding my son, soothing him to sleep and singing lullabies. He was racked with that worrying cough. We were both exhausted from several nights of little sleep. I was rushed to the hospital with my son. We were both in the hospital when my daughter Daina, was born in 1976. Davis spent his third birthday in the hospital, a day after his sister was born. It was a tough situation, but we joked about it afterwards as if we were having a family picnic at hospital, celebrating our son's third birthday and our daughter's birth. It had been only three weeks since my birthday. It was a caesarean birth because Daina was 8.3 pounds, a big baby for a tiny lady like me.

Daina was lucky to have been born at a time of relative luxury compared to Davis. Friends came with beautiful gifts of pink dolls, warm wraps and clothing. She had a complete wardrobe, toys, beautiful bottles, a nice baby cot, and a nanny to look after her. She was a joy to behold.

While everybody enjoyed looking after my daughter, I suffered from discomfort due to a very itchy wound and a stomach which took time to flatten. I looked bloated and was constantly scratching my stomach. It became worse when my husband fed me huge prawns cooked in tamarind and vegetables. This dish was a delicacy but somehow it made me itchier. I wondered if I'd developed an allergy. When I saw fresh blood and thought my wound opened up, I went to see my doctor. I was told that it was normal and wasn't given medication. I learned later that my stomach had been doused with a tincture of iodine as disinfectant before surgery. This must have dried my skin and made me feel itchy. My obstetrician-gynaecologist looked after me during my pregnancy until the delivery of my baby. I hadn't had a chance to look for another doctor during my pregnancy due to my hectic schedule at work.

Maternity leave was not generous compared to today. I only had one month. Any longer and I would lose my job so I had no choice. Sometimes I worked over eight hours a day. I made a point, though, of going back to the apartment to breastfeed my daughter during break time and at lunch time. The demands of my job must have taken a toll on my ability to produce milk because my milk dried up after a month. I breastfed my son for seven months so I couldn't understand why this happened. Perhaps it was the lack of the leafy green vegetables and my exhaustion that caused it. We had a dilemma because my daughter wouldn't take formula. I tried everything and was near tears when finally, I thought of rice milk. We boiled rice every day with a lot of water and scooped the milky substance before it was left to simmer down to cook the rice. Thank God, my daughter accepted it. It must have been closer to mother's milk. We did this for several days until my daughter slowly accepted baby formula in a bottle.

When I went back to the Philippines for a holiday, I saw my previous obstetrician-gynaecologist. She told me that I should not have needed a caesarean birth had I been monitored closely the way she did when I had my first child.

Chapter 20

Life went back to normal after these big dramas. Daily life had somehow quietened down. I was back at work after maternity leave. My daughter was a source of great joy. A child's smile, smell and giggles were therapeutic. My hard work and my aches and pains were swept away every time I looked at the angelic face of my lovely child.

My son continued to be a source of joy and laughter. He was cheeky and full of fun. He danced and sang whenever he heard his favourite songs on the radio or television. He learned to read and write at an early age due to his exposure to books, writing pads and crayons. I made sure he learnt to love books and anything that would expand his knowledge. My son had a photographic memory and remembered little details even when he was two years old.

My life revolved around my children, my family overseas and my job, an important source of livelihood. My daughter was three and my son was six, and they provided us with daily entertainment. My son loved to dance. He partnered with his sister to perform dance numbers for us. When he heard his favourite songs on the radio or television, he would dance with his sister while we, the adoring audience, clapped our hands.

My children went to St Francis Preschool in Tien Mou. It was near our apartment, so it was convenient. It was a bit expensive, but the only other option was to send them to a local school where everything was taught in Chinese. I talked to my children in our Filipino language at home and they would reply in English. I didn't mind so long as they understood our native language. Davis loved to participate in class activities. When the school celebrated Mother's Day, we were invited to attend. It was a beautiful day when we gathered outside the garden of St Vincent's school. Davis performed a solo song accompanied by one of his teachers on guitar. At six, he already had a distinctive, powerful voice. He dedicated his song to me.

> *When your hair has turned to silver,*
> *I will love you just the same,*
> *I will always call you 'Mommy',*
> *that will always be your name....*

After his heart-rending performance, he ran towards me with a bunch of flowers. I was so touched that I cried. I was so proud of my little boy!

I was always involved in my children's education. When Davis needed a costume and I didn't know where to buy it, I improvised. One time, I made a skull and skeleton sketch on hard white paper and sewed it onto a black cloth to make his costume for the Halloween party. It looked good. His classmates had shop-bought costumes. The costumes sometimes cost a fortune and I wasn't willing to spend money on what would only be worn once.

When Daina graduated from kindergarten in the same school, I was asked to be a guest speaker. I felt honoured. I made my speech and imparted some 'words of wisdom' to the young girls. The young children looked beautiful in their 'toga' caps (trenchers or mortar boards) with white gowns for their graduation attire.

Davis went to a Dominican school when he finished kindergarten. There, his talent was recognised. He became an escort for the May flower offerings. He read the Gospel at St Christopher Church during their first communion. On this occasion he wore formal attire, a white shirt and a butterfly necktie which gave him a distinguished little man look. When he participated in the school presentation dance, I spent a fortune on his costume as a French soldier doll. He looked gorgeous in his French red and blue soldier uniform with a tall French hat. The girls were dressed in the same theme. They looked lovely in their white billowing skirts. The doll dance was a success and earned a lot of applause and praise. Oh, I was so proud of my children. My hard work had paid off.

After the initial adjustment of settling in a foreign country, my husband managed to find his way around. He found friends to hang around with. Most of them, like him, had left their country to find work in Taipei. He was in his final year of mechanical engineering when he left the Philippines and he found it hard to find a job in a country where few people spoke English. Most of his friends in Taipei were musicians working in nightclubs and hotels. He got to know the scene and the type of songs that would entertain customers. Tommy has a good voice and he played the guitar well. He used his gift and skills to make a living. When he practiced his songs every night at home with an A1 boxed instrumental accompaniment, we would all listen. I taped him so we had a record of his voice and our togetherness as a family. Sometimes we watched him perform on stage. My children were allowed to attend the late afternoon show. When he entertained in a hotel, he would go around serenading customers at their tables. This was good because he got a lot of tips. They placed money in his guitar while he moved from table to table. When my husband got home, he let my son dig the money from his guitar. It was like a treasure hunt for him. Tommy would tip over the guitar to let my son find more money.

In front of National Palace Museum, Taipei

Chapter 21

When our office moved to the city centre at Lin Shen Pei Lou to be more accessible to our clients, my family also moved from a first floor apartment to a two-bedroom ground-floor apartment for my children's safety. We stayed in a residential area of Tien Mou. I took the bus to the city for work and by the time I got home, it was almost evening. I had little time to spend with my children before they went to bed. In the mornings, we all left early – me to work and the children to school. I missed our time together, but made sure we spent our weekends together, especially during mealtimes.

We had good teamwork in the office. When two female staff members came from the Philippines and one was hired locally, we girls bonded and had fun especially during social gatherings. We oftentimes had business dinners and we all dressed up for the occasion. One thing I loved about Taipei was the food. You could choose from authentic Cantonese, Szechuan, Shanghai, Taiwanese and other specialty cuisines. I loved them all. The different dishes were served every time we had lunch or dinner parties. Western food could be served upon request. Once, we were invited to dinner at a Japanese restaurant. The decorations and cuisine were authentically Japanese. I enjoyed the food as it was passed around, but I'd never sat at very low benches before or drunk sake, Japanese rice wine. Little did I realise that it was stronger than Taiwanese wine. I was tipsy after a few sips.

On social occasions, the only time they stop pouring wine in your glass is when you place your glass upside down. Otherwise, they continue to refill your glass and you are required to raise your glass and say 'gan bei' as a toast all the time. If you weren't careful, you would end up heavily drunk despite the sumptuous meal. Has anybody ever enjoyed a 24-course meal? I have. Despite my tiny frame, I could eat like a horse. I loved eating and it was just luck that I didn't gain weight.

The night market at Shih Lin was a great place for shopping. It was fun just to look around. There were all sorts of merchandise, from the ordinary to the absurd – anything you could think of from clothing, food, haberdashery, electricals, shoes, grocery to makeup. On one occasion our local guide took us to the red light district where you could see girls on display. That was the one and only time we were allowed to go just for experience. It never happened again because our bosses did not approve. The boys were allowed to go wherever they pleased.

When my husband's niece wanted to go home, I had a problem looking for a live-in nanny as I worked long hours. Luck was on my side because the maid of one of my workmates was being sent home. I asked if she would look after my children. The maid was an orphan and had no one to go back to in the Philippines. She was grateful when I offered her the job of live-in nanny because she didn't want to go home. She was older and had the maturity and sincerity I hadn't been able to find in the previous nannies.

She proved to be an asset. Medy became part of our household and was treated like a member of the family. She looked after my children as if they were her own and looked after me as well. Mealtimes and nap times were strictly imposed. I smiled secretly because the discipline sometimes included me if I didn't finish the food on my plate. It worked very well despite the discipline. Medy had a loving and nurturing nature. My children loved her and were at ease with her. I felt that at long last, I had found a kindred spirit. Here was someone I could trust. Medy knew that she was loved and this formed a bond between us that made her happy. Medy's loyalty and devotion was unquestionable and the loving care she gave to me and my children was admirable.

Chapter 22

I had found a very good and loyal nanny, but a storm was brewing in my marriage. By this time, my husband was already very much involved with his barkadas (mates) and had become a neglectful husband and father. He used to come home early in the morning dead drunk or stoned. Once I refused to let one of his mates in when he came in the middle of the night to drink with him. I was working the following day and the children were going to school.

On one occasion, Tomas dropped to the ground as soon as he entered the gate of our apartment. I was scared because he didn't move. He was heavy, so I called the landlord to give me a hand. We brought him to the doctor and after a brief examination, he was told to go home. I was confused as he wasn't given any medication and I wasn't given an explanation. I later discovered that some of his musician mates were putting something in his food to make him oblivious to everything. His temper and violence became more pronounced. Even Medy was nervous and apprehensive when he was around. Only her love for the children made her stay.

She knew there was no one else I could leave them with while I was working.

During the years of our marriage I had discovered that Tomas could be a Mr Hyde when he unleashed the beast in him and a Dr Jekyll when he was in his best mood. He could be as sweet as a lamb but become as explosive as a bomb when his temper was triggered by a simple remark, a question he didn't like, or even by not answering one of his rude questions. My only way of releasing my anger and disappointment was to be busy. I buried myself in work and attended to the needs of my children. I was active in prayer-meeting groups and took up needlepoint as a hobby to keep me going. My prayer group helped me accept the things I couldn't change. Outwardly, we were a loving couple. I didn't want anyone to know that there were big cracks in the marriage. My job required the best of behaviour in public and that included my family.

Added to my nightmarish marriage was a work situation which had become unbearable after a change in the directorship of the company. The new director had full confidence in me. I handled the confidential files. The newly-hired administrator and his cohorts, however, were political appointees from Manila. Their egos were enormous compared to the size of their brains. They wanted to take over and replace the director. This created friction in the office and fomented chaos and intrigue. All of a sudden, there were divided loyalties between the old timers and the new arrivals. It was war in the office and the newcomers subjected those of us who were loyal to the director to verbal and physical threats.

Before this unbearable situation unfolded, I had already sent applications for migration to Canada and Australia and had received correspondence from both countries. I was tossing up between the two countries. I didn't want to go back to live and work permanently in the Philippines. I couldn't envisage myself bringing up my children in that environment and I felt I had no option but to leave and work overseas. I loved our culture and heritage, the beautiful greenery and natural beauty of our country, the hospitality of our people, but the Philippines is a haven for the rich, not for working class people like me. In the end, I decided to pursue migration to Australia. I made the mistake of mentioning that I had relatives in Canada. I was asked a sponsorship from them. These relatives had their own world and I didn't want to ask favours from them.

I kept my application for migration confidential. No one knew, not even my own family. When I was asked for an interview in Hong Kong, I told my best friend Agie and Medy, my housemaid and confidante, about my application. Agie agreed to accompany me to Hong Kong for my test and interview. I had to pass a test to determine my suitability for work in Australia. Agie paid for her return airfare to Hong Kong, knowing I couldn't afford to pay for her. She was a true friend who expected nothing in return.

Agie and I went to the Australian Commission Office in Hong Kong. I was a highly skilled stenographer and had done a lot of administrative work in government offices so I was confident I would get through. I took the stenography and typing tests as a prerequisite to approval of my application for migration. I was nervous, but I passed the tests with flying colours. I breathed freely after I came out of the building. Agie and I then went shopping and had a lot of fun. We splurged on things we could afford, rode a rickshaw for the experience, and took some pictures. We also dared to take a bus that passed through a tunnel 80 feet below the sea level, after we came from the Victoria side of Hong Kong. We participated in a product promotion contest and won two dozen bottles of Pepsi as part of our winnings. It was funny because we did not know what to do with them. We had already packed for our flight back to Taipei that afternoon. We lined the Pepsi soft drinks in front of the fridge, took pictures, and left them for the cleaners to enjoy.

Medy was kept in confidence about our trip because she had to look after my children and to ward off any untoward interrogations from the wife of a lawyer workmate who monitored all my movements. It was uncalled for, but because I didn't belong to their camp of dissenters, I was seen as an enemy. The fact that I held the confidential files had added to their ire.

I only took one day's leave for the interview in Hong Kong and was back on the weekend, so the surveillance was minimal. I took two big shopping bags when I left my place and packed my suitcase for the trip at Agie's place before we flew to Hong Kong. I did the same when I came back home. Medy told me when I returned that Zeny, the wife of one of my workmates, harassed her by telephoning our house almost every five minutes. It was unbelievable! Medy made sure my children didn't play with theirs after that.

The last straw which made me decide to leave was when the dissenters caused an altercation in the office and threatened to harm those of us who were loyal to the director. They didn't scare me because of my strong faith that I would be protected. The chaos escalated to the head office until some of the officers were recalled to the Philippines. Then the office became quiet and peaceful again.

While these terrible things were happening, I decided to send the children home to my parents. They stayed in the

Philippines for one year. Davis was in second year primary school and Daina started primary. Nanay and Tatay wrote to update me on their progress. When Davis became a consort for the Mr and Miss Sampaguita Village Elementary School Pageant, I came home to attend my son's big day. He and his consort were third runners-up as Mr and Miss Rosal of Sampaguita Village Primary School. It was a whole day affair. The parade and granting of awards continued until the night. The long festivities took its toll on the children. When they were called to dance with their partners after the awards were given, my son's partner was already tired. She cried and refused to dance with him so I stood up and danced with my son who danced with mucho gusto to the tune of his favourite song, 'My Sharona'.

    I stayed with my family during my holiday break and went back to Taipei, leaving the children behind. It was hard, but I had no choice. I loved them so much, yet they were safer under my parents' care. After Sampaguita Village primary school, they were enrolled at San Agustin School at Dasmarinas Village, Makati, a prestigious private school. I wanted the best education for them, so I didn't mind the cost. Tommy also went back home to continue his mechanical engineering degree.

Chapter 23

My application for migration to Australia was complicated because my family was back in the Philippines and the children were enrolled in schools there. Placing them in international schools in Taipei was expensive and I didn't want to enrol them in a local Taiwanese school. My husband was also trying to finish his last years studying mechanical engineering at night school in the Philippines. I prayed that my application would be approved because my work situation had become intolerable. The politicking and stress were affecting my well-being. The director and the assistant director were unwavering in their support for me, but I had to think of my children's future, and I needed peace of mind.

My prayers were answered. Late in 1982, the Australian Commission (Immigration and Ethnic Affairs) wrote advising me that we, as a family, were invited for a final interview in Hong Kong.

I was ecstatic! I told Tommy and my family the good news. Initially I hadn't told them about the application, because so much was uncertain and any information that got out might jeopardise my plans. It took two long years before I received the wonderful news. I asked my husband to bring the children back to Taipei and be ready for the final interview in Hong Kong. We were also required to undergo medical tests.

My family arrived in Taipei one week before the interview. We all went to Hong Kong for the final interview. I booked a hotel for two days. I had no qualms about passing the interview. My children spoke English very well. They had a good education and my husband was in his final year in mechanical engineering.

During the interview, my children answered the questions confidently. I was surprised at the way my husband handled his interview. When asked how he would find a job in Australia, Tommy replied that his family had a pest control business in the Philippines. He could establish this business in Australia because he had studied the Australian terrain. He was able to describe the land, buildings, and possibilities of success of pest control business in Australia.

After the interview, we did some sightseeing in Hong Kong. We looked around at the crowded shops on Kowloon side where food and other things were cheap. It was more expensive on the Victoria side, so we just window-shopped. The children loved taking the ferry from Kowloon side to Hong Kong Island. My son enjoyed the ferry ride especially, so we did it several times. On the way to Hong Kong side we saw sampans, boats sometimes used as floating houses. We also rode a rickshaw and took pictures.

Tommy and the children went back to the Philippines while we waited for the result of our final interview. After a few months, I received approval for our migration to Australia. I told my husband who was in the Philippines that we were leaving.

I resigned from my position as confidential secretary to the director. He and the assistant director declined to sign my resignation unless I gave a valid reason for leaving. I told them the truth – that my family and I had been approved for migration to Australia. None of my workmates knew. It was only then that I advised my parents and siblings that we were definitely migrating to Australia. My resignation was finally approved despite the misgivings of our director as it was hard for him to find someone to trust with the confidential files. The factions that the other staff members created generated a tapestry of intrigue, thirst for power and deceit.

It tore my heart to leave the good people I worked with, but the future of my children was foremost in my mind. The workplace was not the atmosphere I wanted to work in, even though it provided a good income for my family. I took my personal effects back to the Philippines, separating some things to be shipped straight to Australia. We had around three months from the time our visas were granted to arrive in Australia. I had to make a quick decision to find temporary accommodation when we arrived.

It was like landing on a desert island. I didn't know anyone in Australia. I had set aside funds for our initial settlement and because of my qualifications I was confident that I could find a job easily. My husband had a very good knowledge of pest control business so he was also confident he could find work.

I had already told Medy, my housekeeper and the children's nanny, that I couldn't take her with me to Australia. I suggested she might like to go to my family in the Philippines or stay on in Taipei. She told me then that her friend had introduced her to someone who was keen on her while my children were away. I smiled in surprise at the turn of events. I met the gentleman in question, and with my broken Mandarin, I was able to make conversation with Mr Chen. He turned out to be an honest and hard-working man. He was a taxi driver. He was poor but had a good heart. For Medy, it didn't matter who he was as long as his intentions were honest. For me, I was happy that Medy was blessed to have met a man who wanted to marry her.

We organised a simple wedding before my family went back to the Philippines. My son was the ring-bearer, and my daughter was the flower girl. I was the principal sponsor. The wedding was attended by Medy's close friend, Chen's best man and us, representing Medy's family. I asked a kind elderly male workmate who was close to the director to give Medy away. It was a simple, but joyous occasion celebrated with a sumptuous lunch. I was happy about Medy's new-found happiness. I didn't have to worry about her even though I was leaving. She had a husband to look after her and they had each other.

During the last month of my stay in Taipei, I attended to the return of my personal effects to the Philippines, having already marked the ones to be shipped directly to Australia. I left Taipei at the end of November 1982. I went back to the Philippines and attended to important things that needed to be done before our final departure. I also took my important documents and mementoes.

In all, I worked and stayed in Taipei for over six years. The experience had taught me a lot and brought forth wisdom and courage. It had been a fulfilling but a difficult journey. Through the years, I was busy with work and raising two young children, but the experience had made me emotionally and financially stable. I know this seems paradoxical because of my marital problems and the stressful work situation, but being a mother gave me that balance. Prayer group meetings also helped me develop spiritual strength. We had a lot of social functions, so I interacted with local people and made good friends with some families who embraced us with open arms.

Chapter 24

When I came home from Taipei to finalise matters before our departure to Australia, I made enquiries with friends and relatives who could help us settle in Australia. I didn't know anyone in Australia and had nowhere to stay when we arrived. It was especially daunting because I was bringing the children.

It was just my luck that my friend Agie, who accompanied me to Hong Kong during my initial interview, had gone back to the Philippines permanently. We stayed in touch during the intervening years. I asked her if she knew anyone in Sydney who could help us with a few days' accommodation while my husband and I looked for work. Agie contacted her college friend Gilda (nicknamed Geng) and asked her to help us.

Agie's friend asked her brother-in-law George if he and his family could put us up temporarily. They owned a house in Penshurst, a suburb of Sydney. Geng explained our circumstances and that my family and I would not be a burden because I had savings to get us through the initial settlement. George and his family agreed. We later found out that this family helped a lot of Filipinos during arrival and settlement in Australia. They were a truly Christian family who didn't hesitate to lend a hand.

I also contacted an Italian friend whom I met in Taipei to recommend a place where my family and I could stay. There were no emails or mobile phones at the time. Everything was done via correspondence, which took almost a week each way. He gave us advice on where to go and what to expect when we arrived. He was an engineer who worked at Transfield Seven Hills at the time. He made suggestions about where to find cheap accommodation in Sydney. He worked a long way from the city and he said it would be inconvenient to travel from there every day while job hunting. There was also the schooling of the children to consider.

I was confident that my husband and I would find a job quickly. I asked for guidance in prayers to help us in this big undertaking. I borrowed the money for my husband's airfare from Agie, with a promise to repay her.

When everything was all set, we said goodbyes. Our house was left in the care of my parents, brothers and sisters who lived there during our absence while I continued paying the mortgage. We spent our last Christmas with relatives and friends and in February 1983, we arrived in Australia, a foreign place with no known friends or relatives.

When we arrived in Australia, I was exhausted. To make matters worse, my period arrived on our day of departure. I felt aches and pains all over my body. The stress of organising everything, packing and sorting out of things we needed to bring and the things we needed to leave behind had been draining. I had to look after the needs of my children too. Upon our arrival in Australia George, Geng's brother-in-law, was at the arrival area with a rose in his hand. By coincidence, my Italian friend was also waiting nearby, holding a rose in his hand. Anyone would think I was a beautiful woman being sought after by suitors! It was sweet and they were both a welcome sight. I was so thankful that they were there to help us. George took us over to his house at Penshurst while Franco followed with some of our luggage in his car.

George and his family were the most helpful Filipino family we ever encountered. They welcomed us with a true Christian spirit although they didn't know us. I will forever be grateful to them.

I had jetlag and was physically and emotionally exhausted. I wanted to sleep the whole day, but because we were visitors in a house and I had a family to attend to, I endeavoured to adjust to the schedule of the family. George's wife Emily was a very charming and beautiful lady. They had two daughters. Emily was working so she let us occupy the house while she and the children got on with their daily routine. George must have taken leave from work because he accompanied me to the bank to convert my funds into Australian dollars. I also opened a local account and organised the transfer of my funds. This enabled us to find accommodation right away.

George had a very good network in the Filipino community and among his friends who played tennis. Within two days, he and his friends helped Tommy find an apartment in Summer Hill near the train station. There were other Filipino families in the same compound, so we felt blessed.

George and his friends sorted out all kinds of things. Someone rang St Vincent de Paul Society to provide us with furniture, mattresses and other necessities to help us move into the unit. George and his family and his friends' families accepted us in their community. It was a great blessing. Without their help, we would really have felt stranded. I can't thank George's family enough for their utterly unselfish and charitable support.

I was assured during my job interview overseas that I would find a job easily due to my skills, but when my job applications were turned down one after the other, I began to get depressed. I prayed night and day that I wouldn't fail. I couldn't give up as I had already enrolled my children in the nearby Catholic school. Davis had to go back one year but Daina started her primary grade at the right age. After three months, I saw an advertisement for a position as stenographer at Long Service Payments Corporation. To be considered for this job, I had to pass the Public Service stenography test. I gained a high score in the test and a few weeks after sitting the test, I received a telegram requiring me to report for an interview at their office in St Leonards.

I was worried about accepting the job because it was a long way from Summer Hill, but I needed money to pay the children's school fees and the rent. Tomas got a job at a pest control company almost simultaneously. He was able to buy a second-hand car on finance, to enable us to get around. He knew a lot about car mechanics, so he fixed it when there was a problem. The one thing I liked about Tomas was his adventurous nature. He wasn't afraid of exploring new areas. On weekends, he loved driving around so we could get to know our new locale. The car also made it possible to accept invitations for outings with our Filipino neighbours and George's friends.

One weekend, we went on our own for a long drive. We only had a skimpy road map as our guide, lent to me by my English boss at my job. We drove as far as Nowra and Kangaroo Valley, the beautiful southern highlands of New South Wales. The children loved the adventure. They enjoyed the clear, beautiful pool we passed in Kangaroo Valley. It was a joyous time together.

Travelling to work was a daily struggle. I changed trains at Central Station, took the North Sydney line to St Leonards and walked from the station to Chandos Street where the office was located. Before that, I took the children to the nearby day care centre in Summer Hill. The minders brought my children to school, along with the others, and picked them up afterwards. The centre was only open to 5 pm so if I couldn't leave work early, I asked a neighbour to mind them. The day care centre was an added expense, but I had no choice. I wanted to make sure that my children were safe and supervised until I picked them up on my way home. We had codes and guidelines in case of an emergency. I have flexitime at work, so it made our schedule work.

Looking back, I don't know what my husband was doing. He had a job at a pest control company to help supplement my income, but the onus for looking after the children fell on me.

Chapter 25

During my first few weeks in Australia I had an experience I will never forget. Discrimination was very bad when we arrived. One day I was queuing at the only butcher's shop in Summer Hill. I had stood there for a long time and despite the fact that the guy serving saw me, he passed over me several times to serve other customers beside or behind me. I felt affronted but said nothing. I waited until the counter was empty of customers. I was angry and I wanted that particular man to serve me. I didn't tell him how I felt because I had an accent and was new in the country, but I was fuming after I finished my purchase.

A beautiful Filipina lady outside the shop asked me to sit down with her and have a chat in a coffee shop. I told her about my anger, frustration and misgivings. I was still finding my way around. I thought the White Australia policy was still in place so I remained silent. She understood how I felt and gave me some tips on how to handle a situation like this if it ever happened again. I'm the kind of a person who puts up with things, bottling everything up until I explode. I didn't want to create animosity in this new place where I'd chosen to live and bring up my children. We came to Australia to make a different life whatever it might be, and I didn't want to create ripples that would affect my children or distract me from giving them a better life. I didn't report the guy to the authorities. I wouldn't have known where to go. Instead, I decided to stand up to this kind of treatment in future. We had been very lucky so far and had met a lot of good people, but at the back of my mind, I observed closely, keeping my own counsel and became careful with my encounters.

When I got up to go home, I was surprised and scared to see a big, bold white slogan painted on the walls of Summer Hill Station, saying **Asians, Get Out!** I was new in the country and I was afraid for myself and my children. I had no experience of this attitude and had never seen such a hateful slogan.

When Davis finished primary school at St Joseph School in Summer Hill, he went to De La Salle College in Ashfield for Seventh Grade. He was very mature for his age and he travelled by train on his own. He had overcome his fear of travelling on the train alone and I felt comfortable when he gained confidence. I was working and couldn't be a full-time hands-on Mom. I prayed every moment to keep my children safe. I wanted to stay home and look after them, but I had no choice. My husband's salary was not sufficient to support us. It didn't cover the children's tuition fees. I wanted them to have a good education. They had studied in very good schools overseas and I wanted them to maintain the same standard in Australia.

I seldom helped my children with their assignments. Occasionally, they asked questions like, 'Mom, what does this word mean?' On weekends, I spent quality time with them. This was also the time to do the household work. Shopping was hard as I was tiny, and things were heavy, even with the aid of my trolley bag. On Sundays, we went to church. Sometimes Tommy would go with us but usually only for a special occasion like the children's confirmation, or a godchild's christening.

The nuns at St Patrick School where my daughter studied were very pleasant. My daughter was loquacious and very social, so she made a lot of friends. My son also enjoyed school at De La Salle College and made a lot of friends. I met the parents of his high school friends at school events, parent–teacher meetings, and other school activities so we made friendships as a result of our children's activities.

My son's love of music and dancing continued during his high school days. He joined the Rock Eisteddfod dance group. It was a joy to watch him perform on stage. De La Salle College always won a place in school competitions. The biggest performance they did was held at the Sydney Entertainment Centre.

I left my job with the Long Service Payments Corporation because although I was a stenographer, I was assigned to the typing pool. I was surprised to find that secretaries were required to make tea or coffee for the boss and wash up after functions like big corporate meetings. I would never have made a good secretary even if the pay had been higher. I wasn't challenged by my work and I knew I was capable of doing more than filling out forms and typing letters from a handwritten pad or transcribing correspondence from a dictaphone machine. I had to bring home the bacon for the family's sake but I needed a challenge for myself as well.

One day, I walked into the ANZ Bank at Martin Place and asked if they had any vacancies. I was told that there were, but I first had to pass a test. I passed the typing test and received a call offering me a job at the Rockdale branch as a typist. I didn't like the position but salary-wise, I was better off so I accepted. Again, it was difficult travel-wise. I had to change trains at Redfern or Central then take a train to Rockdale. I couldn't afford my own car then. My husband had a van for his business but had no time to drop me off at the station or pick me up, so I had to walk 20–25 minutes to and from the train station every day. By the time I reached home in the evening, it was dark. Despite my tiredness and stress from work, I still had to cook, clean and spend time with my children until they were asleep. Sleeping time was a strict schedule. By eight o'clock in the evening, the television was off, and assignments had to be finished before bed. This sounds like an army camp, but I grew up in a highly disciplined environment and had been very independent at a young age and couldn't see any reason why my children couldn't do the same.

When I became permanent with the ANZ Bank, I decided to take on a mortgage. It was in joint names, but the payments were deducted from my salary. In 1987, we moved into our two-bedroom house with a granny flat and a big garden at the back where the children could play.

My husband had a better group of mates in Australia than in Taipei. On Sundays, they played tennis. We would go to the tennis court to watch the match while the children roamed around. The wives of the tennis players were there, and we all interacted with each other and formed a social group. My children didn't have children their own age to play with. The other children were either babies or already teenagers. My husband's tennis mates and their families used to come to our house on weekends. Tommy was a good cook, so our house was always full of people. We made more friends along the way. Later on, other families joined the tennis circle. My children formed friendships with the children in one of these families. Davis and Daina got along with the de Leon family who had three children almost the same age as them. While we mothers were busy chit-chatting, Tommy's mates drank beer in the backyard.

Davis had a lot of board games like Scrabble, Cluedo, Monopoly and chess and these kept the kids occupied. Sometimes they would go to the shops and play computer games. Davis spent a lot of time playing games, even when alone. Daina also had a close circle of friends. The two groups of friends shared many interests and got on well with each other. The girls teamed up to play against the boys. I had brought my children up to believe that there were only the two of them, so they'd better love and stick with one another. Their bond continued through the years until they were grownups. They talked to each other more than me. I didn't mind as I was always exhausted at the end of the day with work, work, never-ending work. I loved reading and it was a bonus if I found the time to read or watch a TV show with the family. Most of the time, I didn't understand the plot of the movie because I watched while cooking, doing the laundry or ironing.

My husband's tennis group had an annual competition with a team from the state of Victoria. Their agreement was that the winning team would host the next annual competition. One time, we went with the families of the other tennis players to Victoria for the championship. It was fun despite the long drive. We teamed up and went in HiAce vans that seated eight or nine people as if we were going on a picnic. Each Sydney family had a sponsor family in Victoria. We were given one room to occupy while the competition was in progress. The same thing happened when Sydney won and we looked after and fed them, like members of our own family. We formed very good friendships doing this for a few years until some of the members split and formed different groups.

By this time, Tommy had established his own pest control business. He initially serviced our friends' houses but when his clientele base grew, he sponsored his younger brother to come over to help him with the business.

My son's friends loved coming to our house on weekends and sometimes stayed overnight when they were engrossed with their games. I let them stay in the granny flat at the back of the house. I always cooked for them. They loved my spaghetti and the caramel slices I baked freshly every time they came over.

When Daina went to high school at Dom Remy College, she also had lots of friends. I made sure I knew my children's friends and where they went. I was strict about this because their safety as teenagers was my first priority. They needed to tell me where they were and what time they were coming home. If they disobeyed this rule, they knew that meant trouble. When their friends stayed over, I asked them to advise their parents and vice versa. Their parents and I were on talking terms. We knew that if their children were at my place or my children at their place, they were safe and having a good time.

Once, Daina didn't tell me where she was, and she wasn't home by our agreed time. I was so worried that I rang all her friends' homes. I had their telephone numbers and addresses in case of an emergency. Daina learned her lesson. My ring-around so embarrassed her that she never did it again. I had no problem with Davis as he always came home no matter how late it was. His classmates sometimes stayed with us on weekends but he never slept at their place. It became a ritual and their parents were happy for them to be in my house.

I cooked pansit, their favourite Filipino style noodles, creme caramel, chocolate brownies, and our native sticky rice cake. The house could be rowdy sometimes and there was a lot to clean up, especially when Daina's friends joined her brother's group. The house and the granny flat became a camping ground. I let them romp freely around the house and in the yard or play outside the house. If the noise became intolerable, I screamed my head off and they all kept quiet. The only time I punished them was when they broke my curtain rod and tore the bedclothes. I was horrified when I saw scattered quilt feathers, cotton fabric strewn all over the room, torn blankets and a big hole on the wall. The previous night, they had played Murder in the Dark and we could hear them thundering from the granny flat downstairs to the first room where Davis and Daina slept. We, the parents and other visitors, were talking when it felt like there was an earthquake shaking the house, and the thumping of several feet downstairs. When they reached the front room, all the lights in the house went out and we could hear a blood-curling scream as if somebody was being murdered. The lights kept flickering on and off, so I went to find out what was happening. They were all engrossed in their game, covered with blankets, so I let them enjoy themselves.

The rascals were about to go home the following day when I discovered the mess they had created the night before. No wonder everyone had been quiet and well behaved in the morning. When I asked menacingly, 'Who did this?', lifting up the broken curtain rod, pointing to the mess in the room and the hole in the wall, no one answered. They looked at each other in silence. When no one owned up, I sent them to the hardware shop down the road to buy a replacement curtain rod with their own money and let them clean up some of the mess. They went together and came back with a new rod.

This drama didn't stop Davis and Daina's classmates coming over. It was fun when their parents came in to have a snack when they picked up their children. We parents were happy for our children to have wholesome fun as teenagers. We felt safer if they were together doing what they wanted but under supervision so they didn't get into serious mischief. It was extra work for me, but I didn't mind as it gave me peace of mind knowing that my children and their classmates were in good hands. In fact, I loved attending to the brats who were actually lovely children. They knew their manners and addressed me respectfully, always asking if they could have some food. I would leave food on the L-shaped benchtop of our big kitchen for them to help themselves, especially their favourite biscuits or caramel slices.

There were times when I was extremely busy and hadn't cooked anything when they arrived. Chris, whose favourite snack was creme caramel, would ask if I had cooked some when he came. Sometimes I cooked it when he requested as I loved the boys as if they were my own. This closeness between my son and his De La Salle classmates lasted until they graduated from high school.

At Perisher, Snowy Mountains 1984

Chapter 26

I made a point of visiting the Philippines every year when I was working in Taipei. After we migrated to Australia, the yearly visits ceased because we were busy assimilating with the new culture, finding work and establishing new friendships. I was bringing up two young children with no one to assist me. I was working eight to five, so I was exhausted at the end of the day. I rarely had time to communicate with my family back home. It was a difficult and lonely life. We had no relatives and few friends initially. It took a while before we were able to widen our social circle in our new home.

I sponsored my parents and my younger brother Fred to come to Australia in 1986. The sponsorship had just been approved when I received a telegram stating that my eldest brother Tito had passed away. It came on a Friday when I came home tired from a hard day's work. A few months before this, Nanay wrote telling me that Kuya Tito was ill. Because of the stress of work and raising the children, I didn't have the chance to speak to my brother over the phone. Then suddenly, this telegram. I stared at it for a long time. The words floated in my subconsciousness. I couldn't accept it as real. Then I broke down when the truth hit me.

Kuya Tito knew about my sponsorship. He was happy that my parents' migration had been approved and that they would be staying with me in Australia. He planned to follow with his wife later but unfortunately, he was diagnosed with lung cancer. His illness lasted less than three months before he passed away.

The news of Kuya Tito's death was devastating. I felt as if a heavy object had fallen on me. I had never experienced death in the family before. I had a dilemma as to where to leave my children while I attended my brother's funeral. Tomas had booked a flight to the Philippines and was leaving that Saturday. He had been going back and forth regularly, regardless of whether he was needed at home and whether we were in difficult financial straits.

I rang my kumare and close friend Tess for help. Tess's husband Danny was my son's godfather. I told them about my dilemma. Tess was the former officemate of my brother Tito at the Central Bank of the Philippines. She had come to Australia with her family ahead of us. I didn't know Tess when we came to Australia. It was only through Danny's association with my husband's tennis group that we came to know each other. The family lived in Newtown at the time while we lived in Summer Hill. Mareng (female friend) Tess and Danny immediately agreed to look after Davis while I was away, in line with our custom of taking care of a godchild in times of distress. This put my mind at ease. I took Daina with me.

Through my grief, I hurriedly gathered resources for my departure. I had no funds, so I asked another close family friend to lend me money for the trip home. I rang several airlines to find out who could take me and my daughter back to the Philippines at a very short notice in an emergency. I also rang a Filipino travel agency I knew. It was hard to get seats. I finally got an assurance that Philippine Airlines would take us the following day. All I had to do was to pay for my ticket at the airport.

I packed up our things in one big suitcase – no frills, just the bare necessities. I was exhausted from work, yet I had to pack for our hasty flight back to the Philippines. Luckily, everything worked out in the limited time I had. I finished organising and preparing things before midnight. My friend and his wife came with the money I borrowed. It wasn't much, but it covered our airfare. My kumare and kumpare came to take Davis that night.

My daughter and I went to the airport early the following morning. I queued up at the counter confident that I could get my ticket there and pay for it with my Visa card. Lo and behold, there was no ticket for us. We weren't even on the passenger list. I told them about the call from the travel agent. They had no record of the call! Philippine Airlines was fully booked for the month of June 1988. There was no way they were going to let me and my daughter board the plane. I was told to go to the PAL office upstairs. A staff member in the office was very helpful. She searched in the computer to find a possible flight to accommodate me and my daughter. The closest one was the following Wednesday, but by then, my brother would already have been buried. This was the first death in our family, and I was really devastated! I cried so much. I said I needed to take the flight that day. I was expected home and I was the only member of the family who was not there. I felt hapless. We were a very close-knit family and every time I went home, it was always a big reunion for our family. Kuya Tito, Ate Vernie and I were the closest siblings in the family. I loved my brother so much. He was both father figure and brother to us during the most tumultuous periods in our life.

I don't know what happened after my outburst. My head was heavy, and I refused to leave the office. All I remember was spreading out all the money I had over the counter. Daina sat there and cried with me. The officer referred me to her superiors. I saw a tall big guy moving around the office. After a long time, the big guy told me to follow him as he took my luggage. Daina and I followed him to the ground floor. I had no idea where he was taking us. I was scared that he might bring us to the authorities to be thrown out. Then he told me that we didn't need to go through the check-in counter. He carried our luggage straight through to the Customs and Immigration area. The next thing I knew, we had our boarding passes and were boarding the plane.

I was puzzled when we were seated in the front of the plane. Tomas was also on that flight, in economy class. Miraculously, he joined us in the front section of the plane. Later, I learned that we were travelling business class. I wasn't sure if the seats they gave us were the stewardesses' seats or just empty seats. I was confused because I had been told the plane was fully booked. As far as I was concerned, the two Philippine Airlines staff who helped me were our guardian angels.

I stayed in the Philippines for two weeks after the funeral. My boss at the ANZ Bank most kindly allowed me to file my leave when I came back. I wondered why Kuya Tito, a non-smoker and only an occasional social drinker, had lung cancer. No one in our family had died of cancer. Tragically, I learned that two people in that electronic data processing department died that same year of lung cancer, and both were non-smokers. One was his close friend. I was sad but at the same time angry that people working inside an air-conditioned computer room were allowed to smoke. It wasn't well known at that time that passive smoking could kill. Or, was it only I who did not know? I wanted to pursue the matter, but I had a very limited time in the Philippines, no funds to pay people to help me, and I was a working class person with no political backing. This was the height of political corruption and chaos in the Philippines and I was told there was no point of lodging a complaint or a claim if I had no solid evidence to support my contention. It hurt me to know these things, but I had no choice but to move on.

It was the saddest homecoming I've ever had. Kuya Tito was the apple of my mother's eye and the family's beloved brother. A silver lining was that my parents' and my brother's visas had been approved before my eldest brother passed away in 1988. This made it easier for my parents to leave the country. They decided to go ahead with the idea of moving to another country despite their age. It helped them ease the sorrows and pain of losing him, the most beloved of all. When I got home, I sent a thank-you card to the Philippine Airlines airport office.

My parents and younger brother Fred arrived in Australia a few months later. They stayed with us at the granny flat at the back of the house for a short period of time. We had a welcome party for them when they arrived. We introduced them to our close friends, which helped them settle in. Davis and Daina, my parents' first grandchildren, were also a source of happiness for them.

Nanay and Tatay adjusted well to life in Australia. Although they were still grieving, as we all were, the novelty of living in a new place kept them busy. They spoke and read English, but they undertook further study in English as suggested by the government for new arrivals at a school in Belmore, a suburb away. They learned how to catch the train and get around on their own. Tatay was adventurous. He and Nanay went to Richmond, a distant western suburb that I hadn't been to, despite having lived in Sydney for a long time. They went to the Blue Mountains for sightseeing. Tatay said that as long as he knew how to read the indicators on the board at the train station, he wouldn't get lost. Nanay enjoyed the trips. She had the habit of listing the train stations they passed by while enjoying the views on the journey. She could spontaneously announce the next station on the return trip. When Fred got a job at Meadowbank, Ryde, NSW, they moved near his work and rented a flat there.

After Kuya Tito's death, my visits to the Philippines became fewer.

Chapter 27

While my children were growing up, I was busy building my career. I took courses at the Securities Institute of Australia after work. My schedule became more hectic, so I gave up socialising and concentrated on my studies and looking after my children. Tommy established his pest control business and his list of clients expanded. When the business grew, he sponsored his younger brother, Roberto. When his younger brother arrived in Australia, he stayed with us.

Tomas bought a van for his business. He was always adventurous and loved exploring. There was a time when he wanted to drive around Australia. Having his brother to share the driving gave him the courage to pursue this adventure. He included me and my children on this trip. We had a long driving adventure around Australia. I was the financier, of course. Chris, a high school friend of Davis, went with us and so did Roberto's girlfriend. Tomas brought his inflatable boat for fishing and hunting riffles for shooting birds in the hunting area. We passed through the Blue Mountains and Orange, then headed for Cooper Pedy, Uluru and Mt Isa. We returned to Sydney via Queensland, stopping at Townsville, Brisbane, Whitsunday Island and scenic towns on the Pacific Highway. It was a hectic one-week holiday because we had to go back to work and the children back to school, but it was memorable for me and the children. Tomas shared the driving with his brother as I couldn't drive then. I was surprised at his stamina with the long-distance driving. We stopped at motels along the way when we were exhausted. I think this was the last time we were truly happy as a family.

Over time, life had become hell for me. My brother-in-law was a known womaniser and he brought his girlfriend to live in the granny flat at the back of our house despite having a wife overseas. My husband and his brother would hang around with drinking mates. Tommy spent most of his time at the tennis court at Beaman Park and when he came home, he was dead drunk. He shared his money freely but not with the family. We tried to join in his social circle but it became impossible. The drinking sessions became sickening and there was no quality of family life. The situation between Tommy and me deteriorated badly. My family could see my suffering, but they couldn't do anything. Tomas reneged on his family responsibilities and his old habits returned. The only thing he did not pick up again was smoking.

As well as drinking with mates, his money was channelled somewhere I was not supposed to know. At his free-for-all drinking sessions money flowed like water. There was a time when they drank at home on the weekends. Attending to them and their friends added to my workload. Washing up, cleaning up and entertaining guests exhausted me. I wouldn't have minded if someone had helped me but sometimes litter was left in the backyard at the mercy of flies and other crawling insects. It got to the point where I couldn't take it any longer. I didn't budge and left the rubbish and bottles for them to clean up. They cleared up after a few days. In my anger, I threw beer bottles on the staircase where they scattered and broke. If they hadn't cleaned it up, they would have been cut by the shards of glass.

The booze, the neglect, the abuse and the violent anger took a toll on my nerves and well-being. Despite the business earning a lot, it seemed there was never enough money, especially in winter when very little business came in. I paid for the children's school fees, our food and all the bills. Tomas wouldn't let me handle his accounts even though I worked in a bank and could have managed the books. He and his brother spent money like water and his brother often pocketed the earnings for his own purposes. I was never allowed to comment or have anything to do with their business, but they were living in a house I was paying for.

Their drinking mates had a feast when Tomas was drunk. Everybody helped themselves to his wallet bulging with money. Not a cent was left for us, his family. A quarrel always ensued when I asked for money. Tomas had also gone back to his old roving days – he flirted and had affairs with other women. Then all communications were cut off – no financial help, no emotional, physical or even care for the welfare of the children although we lived under one roof. Our telephone, electricity and water bills soared. My fortnightly pay went to the mortgage and the children's schooling before anything else. I tried to supplement the income by getting involved in Amway, but that failed despite my hard work. The marriage died despite all my attempts to hold on even for the sake of my children.

In the eyes of our friends and the public, we were a normal married couple. I have no idea how I managed to smile and hide my pain. No one knew the nightmare I was living outside my immediate family – my children, their former nanny, Medy, Nanay and Tatay. It had been my choice to marry the wrong man. Divorce was not even an option at that time.

My stress was compounded when I got a more senior position in the bank. I became assistant to the manager at a branch. The training I was supposed to undertake didn't eventuate. I was plunged straight into the job, which was made difficult by the staff, especially the one I replaced. She was supported by her friends in the job. I was an interloper and I could feel that I wasn't welcome. I was surrounded by an atmosphere of bitchiness at work on top of my already stormy personal life. I was moved back to the head office in a floating position and assigned to another branch where I was allocated a different work assignment every day. I felt so misplaced and degraded. If I hadn't had children, a mortgage and a family to help overseas, I would have resigned there and then.

When there was a restructure within the banking system, I was shocked to learn that I was to be retrenched. I had worked with this bank for almost nine years. I had never been out of work in my life and to think that I could no longer support my children made me feel desperate. I was lost in a tangle of emotional, financial and family struggles. I had a feeling of dread and lived like a zombie. It was as if I had been given an anaesthetic because I couldn't feel anything.

Chapter 28

When I received the small retrenchment package in 1993, I invested most of it in a superannuation rollover fund and set some aside in a term deposit for Davis and Daina's eighteenth and twenty-first birthday celebrations.

I also used some of the money to go overseas with my friend, Lita. She was the mother of Andre, one of the boys Davis went to school with. Lita and I had grown close through school activities and on occasional family visits. They lived a few streets away when we lived in Summer Hill. I was hesitant to go overseas at first but decided to go at the last minute after a lot of thinking and prodding from my parents, my children and the rest of my family. I was on the brink of a breakdown. At the time, travel to the US and Europe was cheap. I took minimal spending money. I had to be careful with my finances until I got another job.

Lita and I went to Los Angeles and stayed with her friends, who took us around. We spent an entire day at Universal Studios. I enjoyed it tremendously. I was like a child exploring new lands. We also went to Los Angeles clothes factories. We made the most of our two-day stay. From there we went to New Jersey and stayed with a distant relative of Lita's. We then took the bus to New York. My lawyer friend Ann, who was one of my bosses at the Department of Justice in the Philippines, lived in New York. She was also my daughter's godmother. Ann gave us a tour of New York City. We first went to Staten Island by ferry. I have pictures of the Twin Towers in the background as we were leaving for Atlantic City, New Jersey. We spent the day at Taj Mahal casino owned by Donald Trump. We were given complimentary dollar tokens to use in the slot machines upon our entry to the casino. When my dollars went down to $12, I went outside and walked on the boardwalk while my friends were busy playing in the casino. I wanted to save my remaining dollars, so I bought a polyester multi-coloured light silk jacket as a souvenir. I enjoyed a stroll along the boardwalk, taking in the sights, before going back to find my friends.

When we went back to the mainland, we walked from lower to mid-Manhattan. My goodness! My feet ached and I had huge blisters. I didn't realise we would be walking that far and hadn't worn suitable shoes. Ann took us to the ground floor where the first attempt was made to blow up the World Trade Building. We continued walking through the famous areas of Manhattan. It was dark so I didn't get good pictures of landmarks like the Rockefeller Building, Saint Patrick's Cathedral where the former First Lady Jackie Onassis used to go.

We saw a Broadway show and walked outside the Apple building where the New Year's Eve countdown is held. We stayed overnight at Ann's house in Flushing, New York. The following day, we went back to New Jersey to catch our flight to Berlin.

We stayed with Lita's sister in Berlin. Des (Lourdes' nickname) was a librarian married to Gerhard, a German national. They had a daughter named Bella. Gerhard and Des' house was nice and quiet with a small garden in the front. I loved reading and enjoying the sunshine in their peaceful garden. Their cosy house had an underground pantry stocked with food. There were two big freezers and two big refrigerators. Shelves on the wall were stocked with food – canned goods, bottles of condiments, rice, oil – everything you need for cooking, enough to feed an entire flock of people. Opa, Gerhard's father, also had a complete set of tools in the basement. He was a wonderful Mr Fix-it.

Oma, Gerhard's mother, was nice and cuddly. When we went out to dinner with Gerhard's family and a friend, Oma suggested I taste German lager. The beer was superb, so different from other beer I'd had. Their mugs were huge and because I was tiny, I couldn't finish a mug no matter how good it was. I was tipsy but happy with the camaraderie and the new experience. When I went shopping and saw the ceramic mugs with the Berlin insignia, I bought two different ones as souvenirs – one for my father and one for Tomas. The train station was walking distance from Des's house, so Lita and I walked there when we went to the city. I got hold of an English map of Berlin that showed the train stops so I was able to go around on my own even though I couldn't speak German. I was fascinated by the array of bicycles parked at the side of the train station and impressed at how orderly they were. It's a very healthy means of transport, a good way to exercise and there's no pollution. The bicycles had their own lane beside the footpath. One time, I was walking nonchalantly on the pavement when I heard the faint sound of a bell. I ignored it. Lita pulled me aside, telling me I was on the bicycle path. Having a bicycle lane next to the footpath was new to me. People in Europe ate only one main meal a day. I almost collapsed as I was used to eating three square meals a day, even though I was tiny. We had food in the morning and lunchtime, but for me, they were snacks. The main meal was in the evening, but I wasn't used to eating large meals at night. I devised a means of appeasing my hunger. I remembered a place where Lita had taken me one day, an alley with stalls where we could buy sausages with sauce to dip them in. They were delicious. I tried two types – a white one called Weisswurst and bratwurst, a big brown one.

While everyone was busy doing their own thing one morning, I called out that I was going out to explore the city on my own. I assured them I had my map and that I would ring in case I got lost. I got off at the station where I thought the sausage place would be, walked in that direction and bingo, I found it. I bought some sausages in a white cardboard box with mustard and tomato sauce container to dip them in. I was in a throng of strangers standing around, enjoying sausages on the street with a common camaraderie. No one seemed to notice me, an Asian, mingling with them. Maybe they were used to seeing tiny brown women. I moved like a little mouse drifting from one place to the other. I explored nearby stores and found some little things to buy as souvenirs with my euro notes and coins. I was confident, exploring the place on my own. When I came back, Des asked me if I was hungry. I said no, smiling secretly because of those sausages, but I couldn't tell her. I thought it might offend her if she knew what I had eaten, especially knowing that they had stacks of food in the freezer. It was one of my naughty days.

I had left it too late to book a flight to Rome with Lita and Des so I stayed behind for two days in Berlin. Gerhard, Des's husband, gave me a tour of the city. He drove me to historical places and told me the significance and story of each place. We went to Potsdam Square. The Berlin Wall had been dismantled a few years earlier but when we were there, there were still chunks of the wall with graffiti on it. I saw the building where our Philippine national hero, Dr Jose P Rizal, studied in Berlin. I have a photo standing with the small plaque of the school on the background. I didn't know that Dr Jose P Rizal had lived in Berlin. He was a well-educated and well-travelled martyr who was executed by the Spaniards on 30 December 1896, charged with rebellion and sedition. He used the power of his pen to express his disapproval of colonial rule. He wrote *Noli Me Tangere* (Touch Me Not) and *El Filibusterismo* (The Rebel), which exposed the cruelties of the Spanish against the Filipinos. *Noli Me Tangere* was one of my favourite books when I was in high school. *El Filibusterismo* was a bit heavy for me. I was unaware that we weren't allowed to read it when I studied at the friar-run University of Santo Tomas.

From Potsdam, Gerhard took me to Cecilienhof Schlos, where the peace treaty was signed between Winston Churchill and the Allies. It was also the place where they agreed to divide Berlin into East and West. We also went to Orangerie Schloss. Big trees were taken to the Orangerie Palace during winter to protect them from the cold.

Gerhard took me to Oranienburg, one of the Nazi concentration camps from World War II. I was surprised that the compound was only a short distance from a block of units. The roads were made of cobblestones. The prisoners had little chance of escape. The compound had a second wall a few metres from the original wall. Any escapee could be seen from the guard posts on top of the walls. There were around nine guard posts within the compound.

The barbed wire was still visible on the flattened surface, even after all the years that had passed since the war. The 'freezer' still emitted a cold draught. How did it retain its coldness after all those passing years, I wondered. There were exhibits of dissected human parts as well as the prisoners' uniforms. I stopped exploring when I reached the small cubicles where the prisoners were kept in solitary confinement. I had goose bumps when I looked around. I could see the horrible conditions in those very tiny cubicles where the prisoners were imprisoned. I almost vomited. I asked Gerhard to turn back. The place was eerie, even during the day. I wondered whether the people who occupied the flats outside the compound, a three to four storey level, had seen it all – the atrocities that happened during the war, the gunfire, the wailing, the moans. Or were the occupants soldiers?

It was a privilege to have passed along the roads of history and I was grateful for Gerhard's kindness in showing me around.

Gerhard took me around the city again the following day. We passed through the Brandenburg Gate, went to the Alexanderplatz tower with Bella, his teenage daughter, and to an open-air café. I loved the café atmosphere. I could see the beautiful sights of Berlin while relaxing. I was fascinated by the size of the castles, especially Charlottenburg castle. Most of all, I loved the different types of German sausages and malt beer.

When Lita and Des returned from Rome, we went to watch the opera *Salome*. Berlin is noted for its musical theatre and has several opera houses. *Salome* was the first opera I had seen. It was not in a conventional opera house but in an open space with huge tents to accommodate performers on stage and the audience. It was held at the front of the Deutsche

Oper. When we entered the tent, stickers were placed on our cheeks. It was good fun. They performed vaudeville antics which fascinated me. It reminded me of my youth. We watched circuses like these in tents during fiesta festivals in Janiuay, my hometown. It was at such a festival in the early 1950s that I fell ill after the merry-go-round ride. We enjoyed the beautiful opera and had dinner afterwards.

Our next trip was Schönhagen, to the south of Berlin, where we watched the air show from the airfield. It was another first for me and I felt blessed to have friends who took the time to show us around. We also went to Aachen, in the west of Germany. On the way, we passed fields of beautiful blue flowers on both sides of the highway, covered with morning mist. I didn't know such beauty existed. I had no camera powerful enough to capture the essence of such beauty.

Aachen was a long drive from Berlin. We got lost along the way and ended up crossing the border between Luxembourg and Germany. They scared me by saying I would be detained because I had no identity or passport with me. I had left my passport at Gerhard's place because I thought it would be safer there. I knew there were no longer any border checks between European nations. Cross-border patrols were only a formality so I didn't really believe them, but I was concerned anyway because I was a foreigner. At the Luxembourg guard post, the guard saluted us. Gerhard asked for directions to Aachen. The guard was polite and gave us directions so off we went. No interrogations, documentation or body search!

In Aachen I saw the towering old church with spires peaking high in the sky. I was surprised that there were churches this old in Germany. Pardon my ignorance, but I couldn't understand how a Christian country could have participated in the annihilation of the Jews. We attended a special performance of a Filipino singer, the famous and voluptuous Pilita Corrales. She was the reason we went to Aachen – to see her in person and watch her perform in a foreign land. She looked beautiful, despite her advanced years. She was more at ease and approachable in a foreign land, not surrounded by throngs of bodyguards like in the Philippines.

Lita and I stayed in Berlin for a month. I had been retrenched and was in no hurry to go back to reality – the stress of my disastrous marriage and the difficulty of finding another job. Lita also wanted to relax before going back to work. She always travelled overseas once a year to unwind. Sometimes she went to stay with her sister in Aruba. It was a relaxing month for me. I forgot my anxieties, pains and sorrows. Being there with wonderful friends and their families gave me a new perspective. Lita had a heart of gold and must have been a guardian angel sent to help me. She lived up to the name she was christened with – Angelita.

We went for a few days to Sweden to visit Tipin, one of Lita's sisters, and her children. Lita and her sisters are very good cooks. Tipin baked a delicious rye bread with lots of seeds. She soaked the ingredients overnight and baked the following morning. It was the first time I had tasted this kind of bread, home-made and freshly baked with lots of goodness.

I was told that in Sweden the sun never sets in midsummer. It was true because at midnight the sun was still up and we had to draw the blinds. When we went out the following day, I wondered why all the vehicles had fog lights in the bright daylight. It was summer and the day was bright so there was no need for headlights. Tipin explained that this was a traffic regulation – all vehicles were equipped with automatic fog lights that turned on when the engine started. If the fog lights weren't on, the driver could be booked. Sweden has thick fogs during winter and fatal accidents could happen if anyone forgot to turn on their fog lights.

From Sweden, we returned to Germany and then flew to London to catch our flight to New Jersey. From there, we caught a plane to Los Angeles for our return flight to Sydney. Tomas and the children were at the airport to pick us up when we arrived. This overseas holiday may have saved my life because when I came back, tragedy hit me hard.

Chapter 29

When I got home, I knew immediately that something was wrong.

Inside the house everything was tumultuous, as if a bomb had exploded. No one had tidied the mess scattered around. My marriage had gone from bad to worse. I received a Notice of Divorce instigated by Tomas stating that we had not been living together for one year. It turned out that my husband had impregnated a woman of his own religious sect and had to marry her. So far as his sect was concerned, our marriage seemed to be null and void.

I hired a lawyer to protect the interests of my children and my interest in our house that I was paying for. Tomas asked that our house in the Philippines be transferred to him as part of the property settlement, although he had never paid a cent for that property. I agreed so he would relinquish his interest in our current house and let my children stay with me.

Tomas tried several times to convert me and the children to the Iglesia ni Cristo sect, but I refused. I had no need to convert. The ethos and beliefs I had been brought up with had guided me through thick and thin throughout my life. Why would I convert to a belief that told me only they can be saved when I can see they are the ones doing evil? If I had been the one who cheated on Tomas, I could have been killed.

In a way, I was glad that the marriage was over because it meant an end of living with his violent tantrums and verbal abuse. He was jealous if I even talked to another man. I guess I should be thankful that this happened because it meant freedom for me – from him and his family. No wonder he used to disappear for months without telling us his whereabouts. He was in the Philippines having a liaison with another woman. This necessitated him to divorce and marry the woman, according to their religion. I wondered why he cried at night in bed and wouldn't touch me. His conscience must have weighed heavily on him. Tomas and his brother continued to live in my house despite the divorce proceedings. They had nowhere else to go. Tomas later agreed to leave at the final stage of the divorce. His brother Roberto and his girlfriend continued to live in the granny flat at the back of the house. They weren't paying rent and I was the one paying the mortgage. I asked my lawyer to issue a sheriff's writ to evict them if they didn't leave within a stipulated period of time.

When the end of our marriage was final in 1993, I felt relieved because it was a deliverance for me. I had a husband on paper and in name only, but no husband in real life – everything was absent from the marriage I believed in. He was very jealous, yet he was the one womanising and neglecting us. I was angry because everyone behaved as if I was there for their convenience. When I was sick and asked Tomas and his brother to take me to the doctor, they just looked at me and left without a word. How cruel was that? It had been a long time of suffering – 21 years of living at the edge of a horrible marriage. He had been irresponsible even when we were in Taipei. I was the breadwinner and decision-maker, but I was subject to his drunken, violent outbursts. There were times when he could be sweet when sober but became a devil when under the influence of alcohol. I did what I could do to make the marriage work although the love was gone. I tried several times to get away from him, but he became more violent. He would rather see me dead rather than let me leave him. I kept hoping and praying that he would change for the sake of the children.

Centacare and other counselling agencies couldn't do anything to help me because my husband wasn't willing to go into counselling. He said, 'You are the one with a problem, not me.' The terror of his volatile personality caused so much agony that it affected my health. I learned through years of our marriage how to handle his violent outbursts to protect myself and my children. I prayed hard and this must have saved me. There were times when his violence couldn't be contained, but afterwards he was remorseful. I felt that he wouldn't really kill me, but he made sure that I was scared and wouldn't attempt to escape. If I hadn't had the children, I wouldn't have hesitated to go but I couldn't take that risk because my children and family depended on me.

After five long months of unending job applications, I finally got hired at the Advance Bank call centre in North Sydney. My work as a telephone customer service representative didn't ease my stress because some customers were abusive. I was also assigned shift work, which entailed rostered working hours. Sometimes I was rostered on Sunday, the day allotted for church. This was the only time I could find peace – in prayer. Sometimes, even prayers couldn't sustain me. It was hard to remove the anguish from my heart. I felt as if a sword was permanently lodged there. I really had no one to turn to except my great faith and devotion. I was dying physically and emotionally. I was on the border of sanity and insanity and to this day, I thank the Lord for sustaining me and giving me the strength despite several times when I almost gave up on life.

I was very busy with work and with my Amway business. It helped me with personal development and through association with a lot of successful people. My uplines, Kevin and Liz, were very supportive. My work and social activities made me forget my problems. I was dead tired when I get home. The motivational tapes I listened to and the seminars and big events I attended boosted my self-development. These gave me a chance to redirect my mind towards something useful and to aim for something better.

My stress at work was alleviated when changes were made in my department. The acting manager grouped us telemarketers together in one room. We were a bunch of six – two English, one Irish, one Scottish, one Australian and me, a Filipino-Australian. My four new workmates had come to Sydney on working holidays. Cathy from Essex was young and amusing. She christened me Noz MacNozz. She and her friends – blue-eyed Simon, John the 'bandit', Janice the 'McCracken' and her husband – were staying in Bondi but they used to come to our house on weekends. Their favourite game was a card game called The Millionaire. This game made them go wild with delight as we progressed through the night and we sometimes ended up screaming as the game got intense or if someone cheated.

We had a variety of entertainment. Sometimes I thought up an activity where we could all join in and have fun at home. On Valentine's Day, I made a heart drawn and cut from different coloured thin cardboard. I cut them in different shapes and wrote the names of famous literary couples such as Romeo and Juliet, Anthony and Cleopatra, Robert and Elizabeth Barrett Browning, Samson and Delilah and other world-renowned lovers. I then shuffled the cut hearts and called our game Pairing of Hearts. I prepared poems like Elizabeth Barrett Browning's 'How do I Love Thee?' Ben Johnson's 'Drink to me only with thine eyes', 'The Passionate Shepherd to his Love' by Christopher Marlowe and other love poems. The aim was to find the heart with the matching pair. Once found, the male partner was to kneel in front of his paired sweetheart and recite the poem allotted to him. Sometimes the girl recited the poem to her love. It was hilarious! We had joyful gatherings on the weekends, and the camaraderie and fun brought us closer. This comradeship continued at work and we became the envy of others outside our group. Sometimes we'd go out for a karaoke night or to the English pub at The Rocks. We drifted apart when they went back to their respective countries. I lost touch of most of them but Cathy and I continue to correspond, if only once a year with a Christmas update.

Chapter 30

Daina and Davis lived with me until they celebrated their eighteenth and twenty-first birthdays in 1994. Despite my sorrows, I decided to give them a big birthday celebration. I had set aside funds in a term deposit for this occasion after my retrenchment. Her eighteenth and his twenty-first birthday were in the same month with only a one-day gap, so I organised one big joint birthday celebration. My children and I agreed that the party would be held on the last Saturday of their birthday month. I told them that I had been saving so they could celebrate their eighteenth and twenty-first birthdays *in style!* For the venue, we decided on Marlowe House in Campsie, a few suburbs away from where we lived in Roselands. Davis and Daina loved the homely atmosphere of the place. After negotiations with the young son of the owner, we made a deal. My children were excited because they were allowed to decorate the place in their own style and motif. The people managing the party were also about their age. I invited my relatives, close friends and other associates and Davis and Daina invited their friends. I helped decorate with fuchsia pink, purple and yellow balloons. Davis wore a trendy blue jacket. He had very good but rather expensive taste when it came to clothes. Daina refused to wear a formal debutante gown, which disappointed me, but I let her buy the dress she wanted. She had always been strong-willed and uncompromising. I was aghast when I saw the short, skimpy cream dress she bought, but it made her happy. It was her celebration.

I asked a friend to videotape the occasion. There was entertainment, dinner and drinks. Daina and Davis performed a duet. They are both good singers, an inheritance from their father. It was a joyous night. Everybody had fun and there was food and drink aplenty. We did the limbo rock, where all of us went under the stick. We were tipsy but had the best fun in our lives. Daina and her friend flirted with the good-looking young blokes serving the drinks and the food. All the boys serving looked good in their formal evening bow ties.

It was past midnight when the disc jockey played 'The Party's Over' by Shirley Bassey, but Davis, Daina and their friends wanted to party on. The young guys who served us were very accommodating. They were all friends of the owner's son, who occasionally checked to see whether we had everything we needed. We had a wonderful night full of laughter, music and dancing. The food and drinks continued non-stop. Finally, I decided that the party had to end. I was sleepy, tired and a bit tipsy. Everybody had to be driven home. We wound down, put the gifts in three cars and headed home. Davis and Daina's friends followed us, but lo and behold, they didn't want to go home. Davis and Daina opened their gifts, had more fun, played games and partied into the early hours.

When I got up after a few hours' sleep, they were still talking and having fun. Amazing how young people can cope up with not sleeping! Some of them slept over and others stayed until daylight. I made them breakfast and it was only then that Davis and Daina flopped into bed, exhausted from the previous night's big bash. I thanked the Lord for giving me the opportunity to make my children happy by giving them the night of a lifetime! It was our first joyous occasion after the divorce. I was thankful that God heard my daily prayers to stay alive and move on.

After the big event, romance blossomed between two young couples. Daina fell in love with Jeffrey, her first boyfriend, and her friend Michelle with the son of the owner of Marlowe House. What a great outcome! I was in good terms with Jeff and his family. He was like my own son. He was a hard and diligent worker and good-looking too. Sometimes we visited Jeff's mother and grandmother who lived in Gloucester. We got on well.

In 1996, my younger brother Frank died in hospital from heart illness. I had undergone surgery just ten days before. Despite this, I booked an urgent flight to the Philippines. I was still very weak, but I wanted to see my brother and be there for his burial. My elder sister admonished me, saying it wasn't safe for me to travel as I might bleed. I was grieving badly as I loved my brother and hadn't seen him for years. I was able to speak to him and told him I loved him a few days before he died in the hospital. Despite my misgivings, I knew that my sister was right. I listened to her counsel and cancelled my flight. Grieving silently, I sent funds to help with my brother's burial.

Daina stayed with me until she finished university and got her degree, a Bachelor of Fine Arts, in 1998. She was a good artist. Her paintings were displayed in the art room at Dom Remy High School, Haberfield. I kept one painting for safekeeping and as a memento. Her self-portrait as a painter sitting on a chair holding a paint brush and a canvass was worth an Archibald Prize. She couldn't enter as she was underage, having painted it when she was around sixteen. She also painted her brother's picture when he was about five, along with a painting of a mother holding a child.

Daina moved out when she found a job. She wanted to live her own life and be independent. Davis lived in shared accommodation with friends while working with World Expedition, an adventure travel company. He travelled to India and South America before moving to Wollongong where he studied Environmental Engineering at the University of Wollongong.

It anguished me as a mother to know that my children had been badly damaged by an unhappy marriage which ended in divorce. It had been traumatic. My daughter developed all sorts of unexplained illnesses. Her skin allergies often erupted and even just a mention of it would trigger her volatile temper. It took my daughter long years of being distant to cope up with her shattered emotions. My parents and family were supportive, but my children and I drifted apart. When they moved out, I felt that all my hard work throughout my entire life was gone – dead. No one seemed to appreciate me or think I was a human being capable of getting hurt. I was deeply hurt and grieving.

Although my son and daughter moved around a lot, living with flatmates, here and there, we kept in touch. It was a difficult time of adjustments and I was always worried about them. When I rang to find out how they were, they were usually busy and abrupt, but I persevered. I didn't want to lose the connection with them. After Daina and Jeff broke up, she went to London for two years.

Even when I was angry and told myself not to pray or go to church, I persisted. I stayed at the very back of the church crying but waited until the service was over. It was as if my spirit and body had their own volition to automatically do these things even if my mind and feelings dictated otherwise. The songs were soothing and without thinking about it, I sang along with the congregation. This devotion had been embedded into my consciousness since I was a child so no matter how much I told myself to abandon it, I just could not. It was like a part of my body – I couldn't just chop off one arm.

No one could understand the depth of my anguish when my children moved out after the divorce. We were all on a tightwire. The tension between the three of us was horrific. My children were rebelling and we were in deep emotional trauma. We were always at each other's throat. I couldn't understand why I was blamed when I was the one who suffered so much by holding the family together during the long tumultuous years. My ex-husband didn't provide for our financial, physical, emotional or spiritual needs. He was absent, a paper husband and father. What's more, he cheated during the years of our marriage. I was a battered wife, an exhausted and worried mother, highly stressed at work and torn by the constant financial needs of my family overseas. I worked so hard to provide a better future for my children. It was the reason I brought them to Australia. I thought that separating my husband from his family and drinking mates would make him a responsible husband and father. I was naïve.

At least, I have two things to thank Tomas for: my children, and our adventure driving around Australia. He could be good when he wanted to, and really bad when he gave in to his moods and darker side.

Davis & Daina's 21st & 18th birthdays

Chapter 31

I missed my children when they moved out as an aftermath of divorce. We made a point of seeing each other once a month and tried not to inject any damaging input, blame, or negative feelings. There were times when we erupted into arguments and walked away from one another. I hardened my heart, but I never stopped loving and caring for them. I wished our unhappiness would end. I was thankful that my children made the effort to connect despite my aloofness. I helped them financially, but it was tough because I had a mortgage and a lot of bills to pay and was also helping my family in the Philippines. I was resentful, thinking nobody cared about me.

Looking back, I don't know how I survived. Prayers and close friends didn't ease the pain. It was as if the whole world had landed on my shoulders. My determination to live for my children made me struggle to move on. I had to be strong for them and my family who still needed my help. The stress of retrenchment, divorce, and looking for a new job, living alone in a house with no husband and no children, took a toll on my health. My blood pressure went up to 185/100,

187/95, and remained like this for almost a month until my doctor prescribed medication to bring it down. I was given tapes to listen to and meditate with several times a day. I would go to a quiet corner in the park during my lunch break to get away from the hustle and bustle. I didn't want to be medicated for life, but I wanted to survive and be there when my children needed me. It took a long time for my blood pressure to go down.

My retrenchment and divorce had happened in the same year, one after the other. I felt like the earth had engulfed me in utter darkness. The only light was my prayers that sustained me all throughout the ordeal. Mom and Dad gave me loving support and wise words. Despite this, I felt empty, as if my heart had been shredded. There was nothing but heaviness and darkness in my world.

Davis had had difficulties in the last years of high school. We didn't really discuss them as I was so stressed out myself. I helped him to the best of my ability and made a point of attending parent–teacher meetings. It was embarrassing when his father was the only drunk at his high school graduation. It broke my heart to see my children suffer.

For me, a marriage ending in divorce was not like death, where the parties recover after a period of mourning. The agony of my divorce lasted for years because there were many people involved who were deeply hurt, especially my children. In my battered state, I grieved as a mother because I couldn't do anything to protect and save my children from the hurt they were suffering. Had I been in the right frame of mind, I could have assured them that even though their father and I had separated, my love for them would never change.

I couldn't understand why my children left me since we needed each other to stand together to face the pain. I felt rejected again and I couldn't handle it anymore. All my life had been centred on my family and all of a sudden, they were all taken from me. I died a thousand deaths in grief. I felt thrust aside as if I were the villain in the whole mess of our life.

It took me a long, long time to recover. I switched off the painful memories and moved on, despite the hurdles. Slowly, I regained my self-confidence and vibrancy. I started to do things that I wanted to do. I explored unknown territories. I discovered a lot of possibilities out there. I travelled more to other countries. It opened my eyes and I became more accepting of my rebellious children. I did my best to live well. My relationship with my children slowly healed. My health and well-being improved. I was a free woman, older and wiser.

The children came to stay when they had no other place to go. I was working full time, so I was able to provide financially and keep paying the mortgage. I adhered to a strict budget, a skill I learnt when young. I saved for holidays and indulged in things I wanted, a kind of compensation.

In a way, the divorce was the best thing that could have happened, despite the sorrows, heartaches and trauma it caused. I had a dysfunctional marriage to a husband in name only, and a neglectful father to my children. I guess it was time that the nightmarish marriage ended. The divorce was the most painful event in my life but at the same time, it was a release from a relationship that lacked all semblance of a true marriage. I didn't want to be a statistic and I didn't believe in divorce, but I guess it was meant to happen.

The bitterness of the situation was painful when it happened, but time has a way of healing broken hearts. It took me a long, long time. Meanwhile, the three of us met once a month as a family. There were a lot of volatile arguments, eruptions of temper, anger and walk-outs but we kept going, trying over and over again to reach a truce and to steer away from hurtful things. We refrained from criticism, no matter how constructive, to have loving and meaningful get-togethers. Everyone was super sensitive.

I tried to move on with my life. I made new friends and was active in community gatherings in Couples for Christ for several years. I became a leader of the Handmaids of the Lord. I was busy with two meetings a week and another four meetings a month counting leadership meetings and annual gatherings. The leadership role enhanced my creativity. I invented, choreographed and taught dance steps to my handmaids for presentations during our annual get-togethers. I improvised steps and completed a dance routine with music. I also designed the costumes for the dances we performed. I enjoyed the fun of being with my handmaids. They loved participating in the activities I created. I gave them the freedom to make suggestions about how to make our presentations a success. Our unique, impromptu presentations always won the approval of the community and it was fulfilling to see them happy. We were often asked to provide more entertainment when we had community functions. This helped me overcome my loneliness and sorrow.

By this time, Mom had moved with Fred and Edna, my sister-in-law, after Dad was admitted to the nursing home at West Ryde 1997. He had a stroke, which incapacitated him. They moved to a rented house nearby. Mom babysat Gabby, my nephew, while Fred and Edna worked.

In June 1998, I met Sam who became my best friend. He was a loner with no family, so we embraced him as part of our family. He came to Australia from England in his early twenties and settled here. He was an orphan, the younger of two brothers. His elder brother lived in England. We didn't discuss our pasts because they were gone. Only Sam could calm my nerves when I was agitated. He also had the same calming effect with Davis and Daina's dogs, especially during thunderstorms. He had a placid personality and I never saw him angry. He taught me patience, and to listen to my children in a diplomatic way. He was very thoughtful and looked after me as I looked after him. We were both givers – it was a bond between us. His passion was playing lawn bowls at the North Sydney Bowling Club where he was a member. He also loved reading and watching movies. He lived in North Sydney, near his work at Australia Post. Sam joined me in my Couples for Christ community because he enjoyed the fun activities on Sundays when we had performances.

My sister Cora came to Australia in 1999 and stayed with Mom at West Ryde before she married Mervyn, my Australian brother-in-law. I was active as a leader in my community when she arrived, so she and Mom enjoyed the activities and gatherings. The community was for everyone, from little children to teenagers, adults, married couples, grandparents and visitors. Mom loved gatherings like this because she met people who could speak our language. We shared stories about these happy occasions with Dad when we visited him at the nursing home. It made him happy, especially when we showed him pictures.

My affection for Mom and Dad didn't change through the years. I loved them dearly. Although Dad could be difficult at times, I loved him as a father, despite his sins as a human being. We had been close since I was young. My Mom was my idol because of her inner strength and the way she glued our family together after my father's indiscretion. She was our rock. She was beautiful in her suffering. When I was in high school, I found a serene calmness and beauty in her face, despite our poverty and hardship.

Chapter 32

In August 1999, I went to Vancouver Islands for a three-week holiday. I was still coping with all the emotional upheaval so I wrote to Ching, my best friend from high school, and asked if I could stay with her. We hadn't seen each other for 27 years but we had kept in touch through letters, updating each other with the events in our lives. In the days before the internet, we never missed our yearly Christmas cards. Her youngest child, Joe, was my godchild who was christened after Ching left for the United States to work as a nurse.

I needed a proper break from work and family. My children had moved out and I wanted to get away from the drudgery of it all.

When I landed in Vancouver, I didn't realise that I was transferring to a domestic flight. The connecting walk from the international to domestic airport was very long so I got lost in the maze. I asked several people where I could catch my plane to Vancouver Islands, but no one seemed to know. Finally, after several more enquiries, I got help from the gentleman driving a buggy shuttle within the airport when he passed by. He told me to ride in his shuttle so he could take me to my plane.

I was delayed by a couple of hours as I kept missing the planes going to my destination. It was raining and getting dark and this added to my mounting panic. I didn't have a mobile phone so I couldn't ring Ching, who would be waiting for me at the Nanaimo Airport. When I was finally able to get the next scheduled flight to the island, I was ushered onto a small plane. I thought there was some mistake. I had the shock of my life. It was a 12-seater with one seat on each side. I wanted to find some other means of transport, but there was none, so I called all my angels and saints to help me and take me safely to my destination. I hoped Ching would still be there at the airport. I think I had missed three scheduled planes. I didn't even know what she looked like after 27 years. She assured me she would recognise me. 'Stop being a worrywart,' she said. She didn't send me a current photo.

Finally, I was up in the air on the 12-seater. The horizon was cloudy due to rain (thank goodness it was not a storm). We passed over a body of water and because the plane was small, I could see the beautiful view below. When we started our descent, I was horrified because we passed through tall trees without any sight of houses or buildings. It looked like the place had no inhabitants. I thought, 'Dear Lord, does Ching live in a very remote place?' I was suddenly scared.

When we landed on a rural airstrip, it felt very provincial. The luggage carousel was small and there were only a few people around. After I took my luggage and still had no inkling of whether Ching would be there or not, I looked around in search of her. She spotted me straight away. I was glad she was still there waiting with Aurel, her husband. She told me they were about to leave. Heaven blessed me after all! I felt safe and relieved after such a long trip with so many uncertainties. Aurel's vehicle was a four-wheel drive. When we reached their place, I was surprised at how big and spacious their house was. They introduced me to Father Kevin, who welcomed us on arrival and led me to a small room on the ground floor with a window. It was already dark, so I didn't have a chance to familiarise myself with my environment. After dinner, I retreated to my room and unpacked. Tiredness overcame me and I fell asleep at once.

The following morning, I was able to look around. The lounge room on my left was big but no one was there. I went to a passageway on my right. There I found Sebya, Ching's former nanny when we were in the Philippines. I didn't know that Ching had taken her to Canada. Sebya didn't look very old. She was one of the staff at the Dwelling Place, the nursing home where Ching was director. I had breakfast with Ching, Aurel and Father Kevin. Father Kevin also lived at the Dwelling Place, a privately-operated Intermediate Care Facility.

I explored more later on and saw the separate self-contained rooms for residents. All meals were home-made, and the residents had nurses and doctors to look after them. Father Kevin was the managing director and pastoral counsellor. He celebrated mass in the community chapel every Sunday.

Aurel said I hadn't changed at all and still looked very much the same as when he and Ching last saw me in the Philippines. I was surprised to hear this but maybe it was true. Someone I didn't recognise once called out to me on a flight from Manila to Sydney. When I asked how she knew my name, she said I looked the same as when she had last seen me in Taipei while she was working as a travel agent. I was embarrassed and surprised. I didn't recognise her. She was young and thin when she did business with us but the lady in front of me had grey hair and looked older. Her facial features had changed too. It was a very awkward situation.

Ching gave me a tour of the Dwelling Place after breakfast. She told me my godchild Joe was the architect of Dwelling Place, but the interior design was Ching's work. I couldn't help but admire the ingenuity of it all. I liked the whole set-up. It was a square perimeter with a big garden in the middle with a fountain and flowers everywhere. Under a big umbrella were tables and sun deck lounges for the residents. The self-contained private rooms had a chintz sofa and lounge. The rooms had a pink motif for ladies, light blue for the gentlemen. The rooms were inter-connected like a self-contained villa, but there was an alley to pass by when they open the door so everyone had their own access and could move around easily.

Opposite the villas was a two-storey house which was a part of Dwelling Place. Ching is a music therapist as well as a registered nurse. She played the piano and sang for her clients who gathered in the social room once a week. One room was full of musical instruments – Ching's collection from all over the world. Ching made a point of getting a musical instrument as a souvenir whenever she travelled. I gave her a didgeridoo and other Aboriginal mementoes. In the same room was a corner with an altar for private prayers for her clients. Ching also had a wonderful collection of dolls from all over the world. Some were from her travels and others were gifts of friends and relatives from different countries. These were arranged as ornaments on the top wall recess of her other apartment near the water. She went there to get away from the demands of daily work.

I met my godchild Joe a few days after I arrived. He was only a few months old when he was christened in the Philippines before they left for the United States. Later, Ching and her family moved to Vancouver. It had been almost three decades since I had seen them, and the godchild in front of me was now a grown, married man. Funny how time flies, how our destinies are woven. It was strange to think that we would finally meet this way. I met Cheryl, Ching's daughter a week later. She had grown up to be a beautiful and a sophisticated lady.

One of the beautiful gardens I visited was the Butchart Gardens in Vancouver. It was designed artistically and was larger than the Sunken Garden at Queen Elizabeth Park. The different sections of flowers and trees were well laid out. As we walked around, I was fascinated by the different flowers in bloom. They were planted so there were always some in full bloom. The myriad of colours was a joy to behold. I spent almost a whole day appreciating the beauty and contours of the garden. The roses of different varieties were especially lovely. I was lost in this world of beauty. I sat under a tree and breathed a sigh of exhaustion and wonderment.

I spent three weeks in Nanaimo Island. Despite Ching's very busy schedule as the director at Dwelling Place, she made time to give me a tour of the island. We went to Vancouver on the famous BC Ferries. It was the first time I had seen boats, vehicles, trucks, and all sorts of heavy transport inside a ferry. One time, Ching brought the jeep and drove straight into the ferry. I was amazed. I loved standing at the bow of the ship because it gave me a panoramic view of the surroundings. There were mountains on either side of the route. It was therapeutic to enjoy the sights and beauty of the surroundings and inhale the fresh air from the sea.

One day, Ching took me to hiking in BC Parks. We took a small boat to Newcastle Island, a small island near Nanaimo. I loved the small motorboat that transported us to the island. I could touch and splash the water going to and coming back from the island. It was wonderful. Ching jokingly asked if I was insured because there were wild beasts roaming around. I was alarmed but I pretended to be brave. I followed wherever she led. We stopped at one of the lookouts and looked down at the clear and beautiful blue waters below. Sometimes we met other tourists walking around like us. After the park, we went to the crabbing area. The regulations were strict. If the crabs weren't six inches long, they had to be thrown back. Inspectors made surprise visits.

Ching and Aurel treat me to a meal at a restaurant near the water that sold fish burgers and chips. The burger was so huge I could hardly bite it but I managed somehow to finish it. It was the most delicious fish burger I have ever tasted. The fish was fresh, and the chips were big and delicious.

One of our outings was a wonderful rainforest trek with Ching and Father Kevin. Some of the trees were 800 years old. They took me to Stanley Park where I saw totem poles. There was a lot of Indian heritage in the area. I loved the massive hollow tree there and I posed inside the hole for a souvenir photo.

My holiday in Canada left me with beautiful memories that were etched in my heart. Ching made sure that I saw most of the lovely scenery in British Colombia. It was great to bond with her again. The only thing I didn't dare do was to walk on the hanging bridge near downtown Vancouver. It was raining and the bridge was swinging. No way I would walk the bridge on my own. She didn't want to come with me and gave up after several dares. She was just being mischievous.

Ching was still as caring and as loving as when she was my high school best friend. The intervening years between high school and adulthood didn't seem to matter at all.

Chapter 33

When I came back home from my holidays, I felt refreshed. Daina was home and I was surprised when I found my house newly painted in baby pink with dark green on the beams. I liked it. She had been bored so she painted the whole house alone. Nothing daunted my daughter.

When Daina finished university, she started work. After she and Jeff broke up amicably, she kept Rogue, their dog who had grown up with both of them. I was sad because Jeffrey was like my own son. They remained friends until Daina left for work in England. I was devastated when she went to London, but I couldn't stop her. She was away for two years. She celebrated her twenty-fifth birthday alone and I knew how lonely it could be without anyone to share a special day. I was sick with worry because we had very limited contact. I couldn't even contact her by phone as we had neither mobile nor landline at the time. She occasionally got in touch with my good friend Catherine, a former workmate at the bank in North Sydney who was living and working in Surrey. This gave me a bit of reassurance, but I still worried. All I could do was pray that she would be safe and that her heartache would heal.

In 2001, Ate Vernie died of cancer. It was devastating for all of us. Davis had a break from college and went back to the Philippines before his beloved aunt died. The deaths in the family had created so much sadness for all of us. My mother never spoke about the pain of losing her loved ones, but I knew she suffered. I admired the way she held on and, despite the sorrows, she could still find beauty in life.

In 2002, Davis got his degree as an environmental engineer. I was very proud of him. I drove to Wollongong with Mom and Sam to attend his graduation. He looked very composed during the entire ceremony, but I knew he wished his father and beloved aunt could have been there. When the awards, speeches and the graduation closing ceremony were finished, we went outside to take pictures. I was introduced to some of his mates at university and a beautiful girl named Lara. I was glad that my son had found a friend.

My son hadn't fully recovered from the trauma of a broken family which was compounded by the death of Ate Vernie. Davis came to live with me at our old house after his graduation. I was worried because he was morose and would sometimes spend the whole day and week just playing computer games. I prayed that both my children would be able to manage this very difficult stage of life.

Daina had stayed in touch with Cathy in England. When she got married, Cathy invited us to her wedding. Daina used her skills as a graphic artist to help with the gold-embossed name cards at the reception. Sam suggested I go to the wedding and visit my daughter. I hadn't seen her for almost two years and he knew I missed Daina and was worried about her. Sam was the most thoughtful and loving friend I ever had. His suggestion made sense so I accepted the invitation and made preparations for the trip. Sam made another suggestion that we take Davis with us, but not tell Daina. Davis would be the surprise package! Catherine agreed to keep the secret about Davis too. I filed for annual leave and got ready to go. Davis had finished his engineering degree, so he was free to go with us. Sam hadn't seen his brother in England for ten years. This was to be a trip full of surprises.

Sam's brother and nephew met us at Heathrow Airport. Daina took leave from work to meet us. We decided that Davis would hide so Daina wouldn't see him when she saw me and Sam. After the hugs, kisses and hellos, Sam introduced us to his brother and nephew. Meanwhile, Davis sneaked behind Daina's back and tapped her on the shoulder. Daina turned angrily at the interruption but jumped in surprise when she saw her brother. She cried and punched him hard for almost giving her a seizure. I told her that she had Sam to thank for the wonderful idea.

We went to Bradford in Yorkshire, leaving Daina in London as she was working. While in Bradford, we went to see the place of Sam's birth. We visited Titus Salt's Saltair Mill, the first mill in Bradford where the best woollen suits and clothing were manufactured. The houses around the mill all looked the same. Alan, Sam's brother, said that Mr Salt provided houses for all his workers in the woollen mill. Alan had worked there at one time. The place is now the Bradford Industrial Museum. You could see the old machines on the cement floor. We also went around the shopping area in Skipton, the markets and canals where small boats travel to Liverpool. It was fascinating to watch the shifting and closures in the canal to let the boats pass through. At night, we visited pubs around Shipley and Bradford. Alan took us to

Harry Rumsden's place to try the fish and chips. It was said to hold the record for the most fish and chips produced – 11,496 orders a day. We also took the train to Leeds, went through the shopping areas and Leeds markets.

We also visited Bronte Parsonage Museum at Haworth, Yorkshire. I loved the scenery, the moors and the countryside. We passed through Cullingworth, Oakworth and Clauderdale before arriving at Haworth. The roads were narrow and small and made of cobblestones. I couldn't imagine myself driving on such undulating curves and hills on the road. Sometimes, when we had to give way at an intersection, the car hung almost vertically.

We browsed in the museum and learnt about the Bronte sisters' lives. We also visited the chapel where the Brontes were buried. When I looked out at the moors, everything seemed placid and beautiful. I tried to imagine the harshness of the moors when the weather was at its worst. I was fascinated by the moorlands, divided by dry stone walling in uniform patterns, which looked like an artwork. The stones came from the quarries we had seen on our long drives. I bought some mementoes and a copy of *Wuthering Heights*. I could hardly believe I had walked through Emily Bronte's house. We also visited Bolling Hall where Oliver Cromwell's war gear and paraphernalia are kept.

Alan drove us to York where the stone buildings were not greyish like those in Shipley. There was variety in the colours here – we saw red stones, white houses, brown houses, and the church spires were cream-coloured. The daffodils were in bloom and York had more spring flowers. We were lucky that there was sunshine the whole day. The mornings and evenings were cold and a bit greyish, but the sun usually came up at noontime. We visited the old cathedral at York. I loved the old relics in the cathedral. It was being refurbished when we went there but we were allowed to take some pictures inside.

Davis went to Leeds to meet some friends and said he would join us later at the guest house at Gatwick where I had booked our accommodation for Cathy's wedding. We left Bradford for Gatwick Airport station. Ernest, the owner of the Springwood Guest House, picked us up at the Gatwick Airport station. Davis was at the guest house when we arrived.

Catherine and Mark's wedding was on Easter Sunday, March 2002. Daina joined us at the guest house after work. Ernest organised a cab to take us to the Holy Family Church at Horley, in Surrey. The wedding was simple but beautiful and the reception was held at the Renaissance Gatwick Hotel. In accordance with English custom, a toastmaster announced our names upon entry, then we were ushered to the reception area. The food and was in traditional Italian style. Mark's mother was a lovely lady who made everyone welcome and happy. Her laughter was contagious. We all enjoyed the food, dancing, socialising and other activities. We went back to the guest house at 1 am, tired but happy.

From Horley, we took the train back to London. Daina was feeling sick but had to go to work so she left us to roam around on our own. Sam and I went to Buckingham Palace. The Queen Mother had recently passed away, so the flag was at half-mast and the atmosphere was subdued. We walked to Westminster Abbey, St James Palace, Hyde Park Garden and Downing Street, where there was a Palestinian demonstration. The next day, we went to Piccadilly Circus, walked around the House of Windsor, and then towards Carnaby Street with its fashion houses. Housing in this part of London was small, with tiny rooms and many stairs, but the rent was expensive.

From London, we flew to Oslo and Davis headed to Spain to meet a friend. The airbus roared noisily so I was thankful the trip was short. My cousin Leni and her husband Gunnar met us at the airport. On our way to their place, I could see remnants of snow that had been cleared from the road. The snow had dried so the roads were dusty.

Leni had worked at the Norwegian Embassy in the Philippines before going to Norway. There, she studied Norwegian and met her husband-to-be, Gunnar. She found a job locally after her studies, and they married.

Daina followed us to Norway a few days later. Gunnar took some time off to show us around. We drove to Drammen, passing some eight long tunnels before we reached our destination. This included the mountainous part of Drammen called Spirallen. There, we drove through the six or seven spiral tunnels of Spiraltoppen until we reached the top of the mountain. I felt dizzy and claustrophobic when the car went around and around the spiral tunnel inside the mountain but when we reached the top of the mountain, the view was magnificent. The distant mountaintops were still covered with snow. Even the river was covered in snow. The Germans had occupied this vantage point during the war. The pole where they flew their flag was still in place. It was a beautiful place overlooking a town on the adjacent mountain. The high elevation gave a clear 360 degree view of the surrounding area. We could clearly see the entire vista with binoculars or a telescope.

At the top of the mountain we ate authentic German tea and refreshments at Spiraltoppen Café while enjoying the majestic view. From there, Gunnar drove us to Viekersund, the place he grew up. It was there that athletes practised high ski-jumps for the Olympic Games. It was cold but Leni, my cousin, had brought a picnic basket for lunch so we laid a mat and had our sandwiches at the top of the ski-jump stairs at Viekersund. It was a beautiful experience with a panoramic view. That day, we drove around 350 kilometress from 11 am to 6 pm. We were all exhausted when we got back to Leni and Gunnar's house. The following day, Daina and I had heavy colds. Despite this, we went out for a drive to Holmenkollen, visiting Park Royal Hotel on top of the mountain. It was an area where wealthy people lived. The view from the hill at the Hotel Park Royal was magnificent. At the hotel, there was a Christmas tree made of real snowflakes. Gunnar said that no two snowflakes were the same size and form. I couldn't help myself. I pinched one of the snowflakes just to satisfy myself that it was real. It was! I could hear the crunch when my fingernails dug through. I quickly walked away in case someone saw me. It was one of those wonderful and unexpected experiences in my travels that delighted me. No amount of money could buy the joy of such encounters.

At the Olympics ski-jump site, there was a simulator for athletes to experience how to jump. It travelled at 130 kilometres per hour. The actual ski jump had a speed of 16 kilometres before the 130 kilometres per hour high jump. It was here that I saw replicas of the trolls I had read about in my high school days.

Gunnar drove us around Oslo, taking us to his workplace and where Leni worked at Europay. From there we went to the Vigeland Park. In the park were sculptured human forms depicting the cycle of life from birth to death. The monolith had sculpted human forms in an interlaced pattern moving upwards on a long climbing cylindrical form. We had fun posing with the male and female sculptures on ground level. It was April but still very cold. My cousin explained that in springtime, the whole park was covered with beautiful flowers. It was a pleasant place to have a picnic or a leisurely stroll.

On one of our long drives, Gunnar took us towards the highest point in Norway. It was a long and winding uphill road and you could see the beautiful sight of the valley below. On our way, we stopped at a public toilet on the hills when nature called. It was around minus six degrees at noon time so my cousin jokingly told us to hurry, otherwise the next drop would be ice. It was extremely cold. My nose dripped despite the thick woollen hat Leni lent me. We passed several farm fields during our drive and I saw nicely tucked rolled haystacks covered by galvanised iron. It was the first time I'd seen a bale of hay rolled and covered with tin. Leni said it protected the hay from getting wet from the snow so the cows could be fed in winter. We also stopped at a deserted beach covered with snow. I jokingly asked: 'Okay, who wants a swim?' We all laughed and walked on the sand, shivering in the chill wind. On our way back, Leni wanted to drive to Sweden to do some shopping. We had very limited time, so we gave it a miss. Anyway, I had been to Sweden where the sun never sets at midnight and the cars had their headlights switched on even during the day. We still had a long way to go back to Leni and Gunnar's place.

Daina went back to London while Sam and I continued our journey. We were going to Milan with a stopover at Munich to see a friend. We didn't have a connecting flight from Oslo to Milan so Leni suggested that we take the boat to Copenhagen and from there, take the train to Munich. We bought our tickets from Oslo and boarded the *Crown of Scandinavia* which my cousin described as sort of *Love Boat*. She said we could find everything that we needed on the boat.

There was duty-free shopping, clubs, dancing, movies, gym, and other amenities. It was a 16-hour trip to Copenhagen from Oslo so we did everything we could to fill that time in the boat. I loved the duty-free shopping in the ship and café bars. We saw the movie *Ocean 11* on the top deck, but I was affected by the swaying of the boat. I felt queasy even inside our cabin due to the ship's movement. I must have slept well, though, because when I woke, it was dawn. It was foggy and still dark. When the sun came up, I saw the beautiful sight of the harbour from our breakfast spot. We docked shortly in Sweden, then continued to Copenhagen, arriving at 9 am as per schedule.

When we disembarked at Copenhagen, we bought our Eurail tickets to Munich where Daina's European mommy, Tita Cindy, would meet us. Cindy was Daina's adoptive mother who looked after her when she stayed in Munich on her way to work in London. It was a long wait for the next train, so we waited at the Copenhagen Station, unable to go far because of our heavy suitcases.

When it was time to board the train, we went to the carriage stand to catch our train. We didn't realise that Eurail carriages went individually to their respective destinations. We thought the whole train would go to one place like Sydney. After running back and forth, asking here and there, we found that our carriage had just left.

We went back to Central Station to have our train tickets adjusted as our train ticket schedule had changed. It was difficult as few people spoke English. We finally found a beautiful attendant, Diana, who spoke good English. She ordered meals for us while she sorted our ticket. She was very helpful and explained to us the way to our train carriage and said to find her if we needed further assistance. As a token of our appreciation, Sam bought her a bouquet of flowers and we had our pictures taken for a souvenir. We went to the station but were told to go to another platform. There were no lifts, so we struggled to carry our luggage on the stairs and ran to the next platform. Finally, we got our train and by the time we reached Hamburg, it was already evening. We had another waited to catch the connecting train to Munich.

I suppose everyone has experienced unforgettable incidents on their travels. Mine was out of character as I'm always organised, time-conscious, and I take nothing for granted. I was caught in an unguarded moment between Copenhagen and Hamburg when our train was placed on board a ferry with a cafeteria and duty-free shops. After I finished my snack, I looked around the duty-free shop. I wasn't conscious of time passing as I was engrossed, looking at the goods, when the lady at the counter pointed outside and said something I couldn't understand. I noticed that everyone had left the cafeteria. I ran downstairs but couldn't find the train. I ran back upstairs and told the lady at the reception counter that I couldn't find my train. I was almost crying in panic. She picked up the telephone, but I didn't understand what she said as it was in German. Clearly, something was terribly wrong. She told me in English that my train had left. I went pale and didn't know what to do. I became hysterical. I was in a foreign land where I knew no one, Sam and my luggage were gone, and it was getting dark.

The lady at reception saw my utter distress. She let me get out of the area, advised me to run quickly in the direction where the train had stopped, and to follow directions I would be given. She made several other calls after I bolted out. Men in hazard jackets pointed me in the direction of my train which was a bit of a distance away. I ran as fast as I could, almost out of breath. I was in a state of panic, criss-crossing the divided train paths. I was lucky there was no oncoming or outgoing train in sight. The men waved signal flags. I heard my dead sister's voice in my head telling me to run faster. Thank God, I caught up with the train. Sam told me that they were about to take our bags down and we would have to wait for the next train. Luckily, Sam spoke a bit of German and had told them I was left behind. I was upset that he didn't look for me to tell me that the group was leaving the cafeteria, but of course, he didn't know that I wasn't already on the train. In fact, it was my fault as I was stupidly engrossed in the duty-free shop, not minding the time, thinking that a whistle or signal would alert us to the need to return to the train. A big lesson, indeed, for a wayward traveller.

We continued our journey, reaching Hamburg and connecting with the train to Munich. I made sure we were on the right platform and carriage number before we embarked. The train left at 22.03 pm on the dot. I slept on and off on the train. We reached Munich at 7.04 am. I couldn't believe my luck when I saw Cindy, Daina's 'second Mom', running towards us with a trolley for our luggage. I had never met or talked to her before. I didn't even know what she looked like. Cindy was a beautiful and charming Filipina who worked with Seminar Union in Munich. She discovered and helped people with musical talents to progress in their careers. Daina was one of her discoveries. She had made arrangements for Daina's singing engagements while in Munich. It helped her earn some money and travel around.

We stayed at Cindy's friend's place overnight. My hay fever was at its worst. My face was swollen and I couldn't stop sneezing. My nose was heavily blocked. I hadn't brought any antihistamine tablets and couldn't find a drugstore to buy medicine, not even a nose spray at that time of the night. The following day, we took the bus and went to Cindy's office. She took us around Munich. We went to see the huge King's Palace surrounded by beautiful gardens. It was a long walk, but it was enjoyable and educational to hear the history of the place. We wanted to go to Austria as it was near Munich, but the trip would take one day so we gave it a miss. (I wanted to see where *The Sound of Music* had been filmed. I loved the movie. I think I have seen it a hundred times.)

We were to be met at Milan Station the following day by my friend Ellen, who worked at the consular office so we did the city tour instead. We passed the Eisbach, a beautiful manmade river that flows through a park and many old buildings, including the building where Princess Alexandria of Bavaria was born. In the evening, we went to a Filipino restaurant where my daughter sang. She had become a favourite when she sang there the previous year. She was known as the black beauty. The following day, Cindy brought us to the Philharmoni (Conservatory of Music) before we left to continue our journey to Milan. It was a hectic schedule.

I enjoyed the sights on the long journey from Munich to Milan. At Innsbruck station I saw the high peaks of mountain ranges covered with snow on both sides of our train. I imagined the von Trapp family from *The Sound of Music* crossing those mountains. I also saw a bridge on a very high elevation, halfway up two mountains where another train passed in the opposite direction. We had a long stop at Verona Nuovo station. The lights went off inside the train and we didn't move. When the train started, it was facing a different direction.

When we arrived at Milano Centrale Station at 8 pm, it was cold and raining. It was a big train station so I didn't know where Ellen would wait for us. We went up and down the stairs and I tried to ring her on the public phone, but I had no euro coins. I couldn't find anyone who spoke English to help me and it seemed that everyone was in a hurry. After an hour of running around in circles, we went back to where we originally got off. Ellen had also been looking for us for the same length of time. I was so relieved when I saw her, I hugged her tightly. Could you imagine being lost in a foreign country with no one willing to speak English and help you with directions to lead you to your destination?

Ellen had a chauffeur-driven car. It was a relief to be picked up and brought to her place. We had a lovely dinner cooked by Ellen's friend. With good red wine, the meal was fantastic.

Ellen went to work the following day, so I went with her to her office. There was nowhere there to rest so I asked the driver to take me around. I wanted to explore Milan on my own. Gerry, the driver, drove me to the old palazzo and the cathedral where all the doves flocked, and I took some photos. I also walked around the shops, borrowing Ellen's umbrella as it was raining. Most of the shops were well-known brands – Bally, Salvatore Ferragamo, Nina Ricci, Dior, Gucci, Bruno Magli, Benetton, Campari, Christian Dior and so on. It was an experience to look at the beautiful displays in these expensive boutiques. All I could do was window-shop. I filled my eyes with the expensive and opulent things but didn't bother to go inside to check the prices. Everything in Milan was expensive. It was a place for the rich.

I walked until lunchtime then met Ellen and her visitors from the Philippine Consulate at a restaurant. We went back to her office where I was introduced to the Consul-General. Ellen booked train tickets for Venice the following day. Afterwards we did some shopping. For the first time, I discovered that I was not permitted to touch the fruits or vegetables with my bare hands. You had to use a plastic glove provided to pick up food. We stopped at the Benetton factory outlet. Nothing fitted me as I am small, so Ellen suggested the children's department. There, Ellen found me a beautiful electric blue jacket which fitted me well. Finally, I was able to buy something! It was a good memento of my visit to Milan.

The next day we all woke early. Our train to Venice was scheduled to leave at 7 am on our three-and-a-half-hour journey from Milano Centrale Station to Venice. It was still dark, so the driver and Ellen's friend helped us look for our carriage and seat number. I wore my hat and gloves which I used since the journey from London and Ellen lent me her eiderdown jacket because it was cold. It was large for me and I looked like an astronaut, so I gave it back to her. I used my new jacket instead. As always, the Eurail train ran exactly on time. I managed to doze off on the train while it was still dark. When the sun was up, I read the train signs to find out where we were. When we reached Venezia Santa Lucia station, I wasn't impressed by the small alleys and market area. I saw passenger and cargo boats traversing the canal but couldn't see any gondolas. I overheard someone saying that he didn't pay $200 to see 'this rubbish'. Sam and I walked around the area where we got off the train. We were in an open market and I was fascinated by the different display of merchandise. I tried to touch the artichoke submerged in water when my hand was almost swatted by a long stick from a lady merchant who owned the stall. I remembered that you weren't allowed to touch fruit or vegetables with your bare hands. Sam chuckled at my indiscretion.

Ellen's friend Rolly was to meet us in front of the ferry dock. He would take us around Venice. Rolly recognised me straight away. He helped Sam and me to the Venice canal boat tour, which passed through all the water stations. As we went along, I noticed that the water was clean, contrary to what I'd read. Rolly explained that the houses in the canal were built to withstand water which sometimes flooded the ground floors of the houses. He added that only the rich could afford a house in Venice. Most were royalty or rich merchants. There were flags in the windows of some buildings. At long last, I saw gondolas. There was one exotic looking wedding gondola. At the last station, we got off and were met by Rolly's wife, Aida, and her son. The family all worked in Venice. Aida prepared a beautifully cooked pasta, chicken, squid and delicious freshly made salad for us. Their children were cooks. No wonder everything tasted so good. Aida said Rolly had a prestigious job in the Philippines, but he left because his family were living in Venice. He settled for an evening job at a hotel. While we were having lunch, he went to sleep before his evening start at work. After lunch, Aida took over Rolly's role as our volunteer tour guide (as is our Filipino custom of hospitality). She guided us through the heart of Venice. We walked through markets and alleyways and along the nooks and corners of Venice. We read in one of the posters around, that 'the best way to enjoy Venice is to get lost' but Aida knew her way around. I was delighted to see the narrow canals where the gondolas passed. I was still full after lunch but couldn't resist buying an authentic Venetian gelato. It was the best gelato I've ever tasted – two lavish scoops of pistachio in a cone. I have never forgotten it. It's one of the reasons I want to go back to Venice – to taste a perfect gelato and of course to see again the uniqueness of Venice with its gondolas and houses built on water.

We looked at shops selling all kinds of face masks in different sizes, shapes and characters. Aida told us they were used for Venice's many festivals. I wanted to buy a mask for a souvenir, but they are expensive because they are intricately and beautifully hand made. I bought a blue and white male joker doll on a sitting position instead. It looked so cute in its light blue hat. Sam bought himself a Venetian hat.

We reached the duomo (cathedral), a huge basilica in Venice. It was the last part of our long walk. We thanked Aida for the time she spent taking us around Venice. We were blessed to have met people like her and her husband Rolly. We had not met or known them before, but they spent their precious time welcoming us in a foreign land. At 5 pm, the rain poured down when we were walking back to the station. The weather changed three times during the day. We were lucky to have had a beautiful day before the rain.

Our one-day tour of Venice was a joyful experience that will forever remain in my heart even though my feet ached due to the unaccustomed walking. We stayed in Milan for a few more days. From there, we took a flight to Heathrow, then back to Sydney. Davis rang a week after we arrived to be picked up at the airport. He had just returned from Spain. We all had jet lag. After a week of rest, I went back to work.

I was glad I had taken this memorable trip because life had some turns and twists ahead.

In May 2003, my father passed away. He had been at Ryde Nursing Home for seven years. It devastated Mom although it was expected. She took the news calmly when the nurses went to the house to tell her. She was alone at the time because my brother and sister-in-law were working. Mom was very strong spiritually and I was amazed at her calmness in accepting the inevitable events in her life. When Dad was alive, I did everything to let Mom see him on weekends. This was the only time I could spare, as I was working Monday to Friday.

She wanted to visit him every day, but I was working during the week and she couldn't walk to the nursing home alone. She had to cross a busy street with no pedestrian crossing. My brother wasn't keen to visit, even on weekends, so I took it upon myself to take Mom there every weekend.

I had taken out a memorial plan at Leppington. It was a wise decision because Dad had a place when he passed away. Mom had also saved money, frugal as she was, a trait I inherited from her. It helped with the arrangements for Dad's funeral. He was buried three days after he passed away, at Mom's request. It was a family affair with the priest and two friends. We had prayers at home that Friday night and some of my friends managed to come after work.

Our trip overseas was a healing experience for Davis. From London, Davis met a friend in Spain, and they travelled to Gibraltar, returning to Sydney together. Davis started looking for work when he returned. I was confident he would get the job he wanted as he has enormous and varied talents. When he was in high school, he was a member of the Rock Eisteddfod. I used to go to his performances and marvelled at his artistic talent. It made him happy when De La Salle College won school competitions. Then at twenty-one, he worked with the World Expedition Travel Centre which I considered to be risky but he enjoyed river-rafting, abseiling and the thrill of the adventure.

When he travelled to India with his group, he was impressed by the sacred white cows and the natural beauty of the desert. He said it was beautiful at sunset and glowed red at night. The peace and tranquillity of the place made the beauty of nature more meaningful. He told us about a momentous experience when the leader of the trekking exploration died. The leader in charge of the biking group fell and hit his head on the rocks. He died instantly. Davis had to gather the group, help them board the bus, and take them to New Delhi where they flew back to Sydney. He was scared but he felt it was his responsibility to gather the group and bring them back to Sydney. He said he was lucky he had the desert map to guide him.

When Davis travelled to South America and went to Macchu Pichu, he described the dangers and the joys of the adventure. He showed us slides of these holidays.

When he left his job at the World Expedition, and took up university studies, it suited his temperament and his quiet nature. He loved the campus atmosphere in Wollongong.

After a few months of job applications, he was offered an engineering job in a remote part of the Himalayas. This concerned me because communications would be impossible. He wanted to go to a no-man's-land, a place I had hardly heard of, with no friends to turn to in case of emergency. I prayed hard to all the angels and saints and the Blessed Mother to help my son make the right choice and to please not send him into the middle of nowhere. My prayers were answered when after a few weeks, he accepted an engineering job in Wales in 2003. I was able to breathe, thank God, as he would be in a place I could locate on the map. My friend Catherine lived in Surrey and in case of an emergency he could go to my cousin Leni in Norway. During his three-year contract at Hyder Consulting, he also had assignments in Doha and Dubai.

When I discovered that Davis hadn't told his father about this job, I encouraged him to say goodbye to his father and to let him know that he was going away for three years for work. Davis was reluctant at first, but Daina dialled her father's number and Davis talked to him. He cried, but it was better for him to go having made peace with his father. Davis kept his emotions bottled up, which was not good, but I hadn't realised things with his father went so deep. I found out that he didn't want his parents to divorce. All I could do as a mother was to pray for his safety and guidance.

When Daina returned to Australia for good, she moved in with friends and joined a band, devoting her time to music while working as a graphic artist. I sometimes attended her gigs. I was very proud of her artistic accomplishments.

Chapter 34

From late December 2003 to January 2004, Nanay, Sam and I went to the Philippines for a holiday. With the help of my cousins, I arranged a surprise for both Nanay and Sam.

Sam had no family of his own. I wanted him to experience the family life he'd never had. I wanted Nanay to see relatives for the first time in many years. With my brothers Ben and Eddie and first cousins Connie Rose and Pinky, we hired a resort at Pansol, Laguna. It had a swimming pool where the hot springs came directly from the mountain. The water was known for its therapeutic benefits. Ben and Eddie took charge of organising the relatives on Nanay's side, and Connie Rose and Pinky on Tatay's side. My brother Fred, sister Cora and I convinced Nanay to travel home while she was still strong and able to move around. She and Tatay hadn't been back to the Philippines since they had moved to Australia. It was a pity that Tatay passed away without having had the chance to return.

Nanay had a strong faith and a quiet way of dealing with difficulties. You could call her stoic, although she also had a soft and loving heart, hiding her pain and sorrows in quiet prayer and acceptance. Nanay and I financed this major undertaking. Nanay was frugal and lived a simple life. She always tucked a little away from the money she received, so she had ample funds to pay for her fare with extra for spending. She was excited to see my younger brothers, our relatives and other grandchildren. Sam wanted to go as well so we booked our flights together. We requested wheelchair assistance for Nanay. She refused initially, insisting that she could walk and was not handicapped. I booked it anyway, knowing how long the walk was from the plane across the tarmac to the exit. The walk after our check-in to the airplane gate in Sydney was long, and when we landed, it was an even longer distance from the airplane gate to the exit where our relatives were waiting to pick us up. Sam pushed Nanay's wheelchair and assisted her. I was struggling with the heavy hand-carry bag full of pasalubongs (arrival gifts) for relatives.

We secretly organised for Nanay's only remaining sister to be there. She lived in Janiuay, our central Philippines province. We paid her fare to Manila to meet Nanay and did the same for Nanay's youngest brother, Uncle Enrique. It was heartbreaking when we heard he couldn't come. Tay Adring, as we called him, was too ill to make the journey from his barrio to Manila. It was a pity because this was the only opportunity for them to meet after the long years of not seeing one another. There was no telephone where he lived in the barrio so I made contact with Tay Adring's daughter who lived in Iloilo. We communicated our wishes for his quick recovery and sent Nanay's love. We were very disappointed. Nanay hadn't seen Tay Adring for a long, long time. We left Iloilo for the northern part of the Philippines when I was still young. In all my life, I had only seen him once.

Iyay Bidad (our pet name for Aunt Natividad), had two grown-up children. They were both married and lived in Quezon City. She stayed with Ronnie, her eldest son. Ronnie, my first cousin, was close to me and always dropped everything to see me when I visited the Philippines. We were the only link between our mothers. I hadn't met Glen, Iyay Bidad's younger son. Tay Teroy (Uncle Sotero), her husband, opted to stay behind in Janiuay.

Nanay and Iyay Bidad stayed in Liliw, Laguna, with my youngest brother's family. It was a joy to see Nanay and Iyay Bidad catching up with each other. We went with them to Liliw, so we could spend some time with the family. On the drive from Las Pinas to Liliw, around 180 kilometres away, I listened to the conversations in dialect between Nanay and Iyay Bidad. I could still understand and speak my childhood dialect. Iyay Bidad said, while looking sideways at Nanay, 'I don't think you are my sister. You are so beautiful.' Nanay said, 'Of course I am your sister. We have the same mother.' They talked about their relatives and their lives way back then. This assured Iyay Bidad that they were really sisters. They had a long time catching up with each other's lives, the long gap of intervening years. They didn't grow up with modern technology of emailing and texting or overseas calls. My aunt had no landline or mobile phone in the provinces where they lived. Nanay wrote to her and Tay Adring, but communications were infrequent.

We were at the petrol station when Iyay Bidad suddenly burst into English and said, 'I don't like that.' We all looked at her, stunned. I giggled because it reminded me of the time when she pinched me when I lived with her and annoyed her when I stopped kneeling and didn't respond to her litany in Latin.

After all the relatives were informed of our reunion, we set out for La Maria Spring Resort in Pansol, Laguna. There were several cottages where we could sleep as a group, an entertainment area, kitchen, swimming pool and showers. My cousins installed karaoke in the entertainment area, while the maids and the rest of the women busied themselves preparing food for the entire flock. Several vehicles transported relatives coming from different directions – privately hired jeepneys, private cars, and big vans. Auntie Nene, the wife of my father's brother who had passed away, travelled the farthest distance with her children and grandchildren in a big van. She was another one who would drop everything to see me.

I ordered the gate closed to prevent interlopers and unwanted guests, but Sam said, 'I don't think so.' He pointed to vehicles still coming in, three more jeepneys full of people. I was alarmed and asked my brother Ben who those people were. He told me that they were Nanay's nephews and nieces' family whom my brother Ben contacted. Oh my! I didn't realise there were so many! Our food was only enough for 150 people for breakfast, lunch and dinner and for the following day. My two cousins were quick witted. They had catered for a lot of people at several family functions. They said we could use the following day's provisions for today and buy more food from the nearby market the following morning. Luckily, some relatives brought casseroles of cooked food as their contribution.

Meanwhile, the relatives looked for Nanay who was inside one of the cottages, resting and talking to her sister. She was surprised when all of a sudden, there was an influx of adults and children taking her hand simultaneously, placing it on their foreheads saying 'mano po', as a sign of respect and also a blessing for a respected elder, as is our custom. She was mesmerised and asked whose children were those and from which generation. I laughed because I was as confused as she was. We were introduced to the husband or wife of the third generation and their children who were Nanay's fourth generation grandchildren. Afterwards, all of them disappeared. I wondered where they were. Then I heard shrieks from the swimming pool. It was full of black heads bobbing in and around the pool. They dived straight into the pool after removing their clothes. We adults also wanted a dip in the pool following all our hard work. I changed into my bathing suit but when I went to the pool, it was still full of children. They didn't want to get out, so I went back and had a shower, making a note to take a dip in the pool early in the morning while they were all sleeping.

This was a joyous reunion. It was crazy! Nanay was overjoyed to be among her own and Tatay's relatives. It was kind of lonely for her in Australia with only one grandchild. My children were already adults and were travelling in other parts of the world. We always saw Tatay's relatives but now, we were also reunited with Nanay's poorer relatives. We had a lot of entertainment. My cousins and their family brought everything we needed – music, paper plates, cups, forks and spoons, woks and kitchen utensils, drinks, pillows. You name it, they had it. Pinky and her husband Odes brought karaoke songs and dancing. Someone brought a guitar. There were games like Scrabble and cards. The men gathered together drinking beer and singing karaoke. My brother Ben scored 100 in karaoke. I was surprised. I didn't even know he could sing. Even Sam tried singing. We were all exhausted by evening. We dropped like logs on the floor and balconies. Others slept in their vehicles, on benches and portable beds. Nanay, Iyay Bidad, the children and I slept in the cottage with room dividers.

The next day, Connie Rose and I went to the market to buy more food. Pinky attended to preparing lunch. When we came back, we had all the supplies needed – rice, meat, fish, vegetables, coconut drinks and fruit. Relatives also brought delicacies for morning and afternoon snacks. It was a time for eating, relaxing, catching up and rejoicing.

Connie Rose and Pinky were adept at feeding people en masse. I left them to devise ways and means to feed us all. I was impressed at the way they worked together. Their husbands, Manny and Odes, were a great support too. Everyone helped arrange the five or six metre table layered with banana leaves. Newly cooked rice was spread along the length of the banana leaves. Barbecued pork and chicken, fish, chopped tomatoes and onions were laid out on both sides of the rice so no one missed out on meat, fish or salad.

When the meal was ready, we asked everyone to wash their hands and line up on both sides of the table. I stayed at the head of the table to lead the thanksgiving grace. As soon as I finished saying grace, everyone helped themselves to the food. Sam and I took a lot of photos. After lunch he told me he'd never seen a mob finish food so quickly right after the prayers. He hadn't eaten but he wasn't interested in food. He was mesmerised by the sight before him and continued taking pictures. I guess he had never seen anything like that. I was glad for him to experience a joyous family reunion, a moment of sharing and also the experience of how it was to have a big family. Sam had only one brother in England and they very seldom communicated with each other. It was sad, really. I was glad we were his adoptive family.

I had never seen Nanay or Sam look so happy. They were both loners in their own ways, but I could see the joy in their faces to be surrounded by loving generations of families who only wanted to make the event a memorable one. For all of us, it was a moment of happiness that no money could ever buy, and it will be etched in our memories forever.

It was sad that my beloved children were not with me. Davis was in Wales and Daina was working and could not make it.

In 2006, Davis wanted to come home for a holiday. I took a sale package to Hamilton Island for our reunion. My children decided to meet in Thailand before the family holiday. It was a restorative time for both of them. Daina was undergoing her own therapeutic healing. Davis took leave from his work in Dubai and Daina met him during his stopover in Thailand. They went to Phi Phi Island which had been devastated by the freak tsunami the previous year. The movie *The Beach* starring Leonardo di Caprio was filmed there. They said the island retained its beauty. The water was very clear and beautiful although some of the rocks had been chipped off by the tsunami. They went snorkelling and enjoyed the beauty of the beaches and the water. Davis was intrigued by the place.

I had sold our house at Roselands in 2004 and downsized to a unit on the first floor with a balcony. I paid off the mortgage and moved to a more contained and manageable space. There was less cleaning. I loved my new place in a big compound with no floors above me. It was just the place I wanted to be. It was sad because I couldn't take Lando, Davis' dog, with me. It caused me and Davis a lot of heartache when we learned what happened. I got the RSPCA letter saying I could visit Lando, but when I rang, I learned that he was already gone. They couldn't even give me his remains. I cried at work and went home crying. I felt aggrieved because Davis' friend hadn't even given me the courtesy of a call to tell me this was happening. I loved Lando. He was my protector when he was with me guarding my house and myself. One time, I saw a black dog in front of the gate in my new place. The dog stared at me and when I called 'Lando?', he continued to stare. When I went to him, he walked away despite me calling him several times, but he turned his head and looked at me as if saying goodbye. I didn't see him again and no black dog ever walked along our street after that. When Davis and Daina arrived from Thailand, Davis was disoriented because I lived in an apartment. It was an alien place for him. He missed the old house.

I had booked our holiday to Hamilton Island before the holiday in Thailand. The children rested for a few days and then we went together. Hamilton Island was a perfect place for healing. It was serene, the atmosphere was beautiful, we were surrounded by water and we didn't have to worry about food. An abundant breakfast was part of the package. We walked around the island at our ease. It was also nice to lie down near the beach and read a book. We went to the Great Barrier Reef from there. I was disappointed as the coral looked grey and dead. I was expecting a beautiful multi-coloured reef. When I asked the operator why the coral looked brown, she had no answer. Later, I found that the colour of the coral was a product of bleaching caused by pollution and chemicals dumped into the sea. How sad! On our way back, the boat rocked violently, scaring me. One of the guides said the seas were rough at this time of the year.

On the day of our flight home, there was news of a storm coming from Townsville. It rained and the wind was strong when the plane landed to take us back to Sydney. It was scary because the runway in Hamilton Island was short. One slight mistake could be fatal, but take-off was smooth and the flight back to Sydney was pleasant. That night, we heard from the news that the storm lashed Hamilton Island right after we left and subsequent flights were cancelled. We joked about ourselves – what was it with the three of us that we were always chased by storms? The storm flattened banana plantations in Queensland and did a lot of damage in Townsville. Daina and her friend had the same experience during the last leg of their holidays in Europe. They had left the Czech Republic when a storm hit and flooded the area. I was concerned when I saw about it in the news but Daina was already on her way home.

We enjoyed being together for a few more days before going back to our separate lives. I was still working, and my job gave me solace during my lonely days without my children. Davis went back to his job in Wales. Later, he told me he was coming home for good. His three-year contract was over. It must have been lonely for him without his family nearby. I was glad at the news that finally my son would be home and not too far away.

Davis got a senior position in an engineering company in North Sydney, and after staying with me for a short while, he and his sister rented a place in Vaucluse. I didn't mind so long as they were together.

During his years in Wales, he seldom communicated. I knew it was his way of healing, to be away from the family, but it was very taxing for me. I kept the communication open even though he seldom told me what was happening in his life. He was offered a job in London, but he didn't want to be in a place where there was a lot of hustle and bustle. He finalised his homecoming arrangements, left his beloved car, an MG, with a friend, and had his personal effects shipped back to Sydney. I picked him up at the airport and his first words were: 'Jesus, thank God, I'm home.'

Chapter 35

From December 2007 to January 2008, I went back to the Philippines. I was getting lonely on my own, so I decided to make the trip. I flew with Singapore Airlines and stayed overnight in Singapore for the experience. I had an overnight stay at a hotel in Singapore as part of the package. It gave me a chance to look around and get a glimpse of Singapore.

The flight was a new airbus, a double-decker. I went to the first deck to see what it was like. Everything was impressive. The stewardesses looked like living dolls in their beautiful uniforms, all slim, young, tall and beautiful. They had the same hairstyle – a neat bun that accentuated their porcelain-like features. When we landed in Singapore, I was the last passenger on the shuttle bus to get off at my hotel, the Peninsula Excelsior. I got out and walked around the area. I found some Chinese take-away stores and other interesting shops behind the hotel. I decided to join a night tour instead of wasting my time alone in a hotel. The hotel shuttle bus picked us up and took us to the Quayside where we met our tour guide. The tour guide spoke rapidly, giving strict and rigid instructions to be observed during the tour. During this guided tour I met Vicky, a beautiful young Chinese student from Canton. We were both travelling alone so we stuck together during the tour. We had a river boat ride then dinner at a night restaurant along the quay. Afterwards, they took us to the Royal Selangor Pewter Company where I bought a beautiful pewter necklace for myself. We went to Bugis Street night market and lastly, to the famous Raffles City Club where, for a minimum of $25, we could have a drink and eat peanuts, littering the floor with the shells, in keeping with tradition. Vicky and I were intrigued so we went to the Raffles City Club together. She ordered a Singapore Sling, which I also tried for the sake of experience. It was good fun. Afterwards we walked back to the hotel. Vicky was leaving for China at 4 am and I wondered how she would cope without sleep. She would later go to England to finish her economics degree. The following day, I left for the Philippines, a three-hour flight.

My cousin Pinky always held a family reunion at her place during Christmas and New Year. Her big compound could accommodate 150 people. This family reunion included all relatives on my father's side from the first generation down to the last. Pinky's husband held a similar family reunion every year. The family reunion was always great fun, an occasion to meet local relatives and those from other countries.

I decided to go home again for this family reunion because Christmas and New Year celebrations there were happy times. You could feel it in the air. Everywhere, people had Christmas decorations in their houses and lavish food to celebrate the occasion. The big companies in Makati, a place as built up as New York, were decorated with neon lights and the main thoroughfares had parol (star decorations).

This time, through a referral from Sydney, I booked a privately-owned condo-hotel in Makati. When I got there, it turned out that the area was not very nice. The hotel's elevator was broken, and I was on the seventh floor. There were no lights on the stairs except the ground floor. The hotel had no generator for emergencies. Luckily my relatives were there to stay with me during the night. It was our big family reunion the following day so my other cousin who lived in Pasay City picked me up from the hotel. I took my luggage with me as I didn't want to go back to that horrible condo-hotel. I ended up staying at my cousin's place in Pasay City for my entire holiday.

I attended this reunion with my remaining two brothers living in the Philippines and their families. The rest of my relatives and their families were also invited. My cousin and her husband always gave the best parties. Pinky was a very good organiser. All the activities were taken care of – the buffet on long tables, rooms with en-suites to accommodate visitors, music, games for the children, and room for unexpected additional visitors. Our custom when we have parties is that it is an all-day event with a non-stop flow of food and entertainment. The event oftentimes extends until the next day. These were always happy occasions and this reunion enabled me to meet distant cousins and spend time with relatives I hadn't seen for a long time. After many years, I saw my uncles and aunts on my father's side, and first cousins from overseas and their families. It was a pity that neither my children nor my mother was with me.

I stayed at Pinky's place until New Year's Eve. It was fun because there was karaoke at the big compound in the backyard, a basketball area and a place where we could all sit, eat and do whatever we wished. We had a photo session with all the family. At midnight, we all went to the rooftop of the three-storey house to see the firecrackers. We only had sparklers because there were a lot of children. The neighbours had successive arrays of expensive firecrackers and it amazed me as I looked around. It was as if I hadn't left Sydney as I watched beautiful firecrackers light the sky in one explosion after the other. After the firecrackers, we went down for the traditional New Year's midnight snack. The table was full of food. Afterwards, Pinky called the children to the compound at the backyard and threw coins in the air, so everybody had fun jumping and catching the coins and then picking up the ones that dropped on the ground. Of course, we adults also participated in the fun! It was a memorable reunion!

A couple of days later, my friend Agie from Laguna province picked me up to stay at her place at the University of the Philippines, Los Banos in Laguna. We were going to Taipei together. We had met there when she worked with the Asian Pacific Company and our families got to know each other when the children were young. Agie gave me a tour around the Makiling Botanic Gardens and the University of the Philippines Los Banos College of Arts and Sciences a few days before our trip to Taipei.

Agie and I flew to Taipei in the first week of January 2008 to visit Medy, my children's wonderful nanny. My children and I loved her. The years had flown but the friendship remained. We made it a point to remember birthdays and Christmas. Chen, Medy's husband, thanked me for having given him a very good wife. He is such a sweet man and Medy was lucky to have found him. They were both happy and had moved to Taichung, on the southern tip of Taiwan where they bought a unit when Chen retired. Medy said she was getting old and wanted to see us again. I promised I would, and this was my chance.

Medy travelled by train from Taichung, the southern part of Taiwan, to meet us in Taipei. She booked a hotel in Shih Lin for all of us so that we could go around and see the places that I hadn't seen for twenty-six years. My cousin Ate Beth joined us in Taipei after a few days. She was a traveller who went back to the Philippines every year for her class reunion held at St Paul College in Iloilo City. Most of her college friends from the United States did the same. Ate Beth had got to know Medy when she visited me while I was working in Taipei. She also wanted to see Medy again.

When we were all gathered at the hotel in Taipei, we had a lot of fun reminiscing about the old days. We went to the places where I and my family used to live and to other places where Medy reminded me that this and that had happened, but I couldn't recognise them anymore. The place had changed significantly after twenty-six years. I didn't recognise the place where we lived, even when Medy pointed out the exact location. It looked different and more commercialised. The big house where we had our first office in Taipei was gone. The landmarks I had known were all gone. Business buildings had been erected in the residential areas I had known. There was now an American School in Shih Lin. The only landmark I recognised was the St Vincent's preschool where my children attended kindergarten. It had become an orphanage managed by the nuns. I learned that Father Beunen, the German priest who christened my daughter, had passed away. (What did I expect when my daughter was over thirty years old?)

We went to the famous Shihlin night market. Medy knew the way so we followed her. I thought it was only a short distance, but it turned out to be a long walk, probably around five kilometres from where we started. I was used to walking but not that distance, and it was the same for Ate Beth. We had several rests before we reached our destination. Shihlin night market would blow your mind. It was fascinating to see all the merchandise, catering to anything a person or a household would need. There were hundreds or maybe thousands of people milling around, foreigners and locals alike, trying to find good things at a bargain price. You really needed to bargain hard to get the best price. I used my slight knowledge of Mandarin that I had not spoken for so long a time. It was always an advantage when you knew the local dialect or were with a local who knew the dialect. Medy was an asset because she had become a local, being married to a Chinese. She had mastered Taiwanese and Mandarin without having forgotten our Filipino language.

We went to Wulai a town famous for its hot springs. At the Gaga International Theatre, we watched the Taiya Musical Dance Company present the Atayal traditional wedding dance. We took a mini-train ride which was open on both sides when we went to Wulai. It passed through a winding mountain road. For me, it was fun, but I hadn't been there for a long time, so it seemed different and not as exotic and mysterious as the first time. When I was working in Taipei, my children loved going there. We used to go up the top of Wulai on a cable car. It was scary to look down as we were suspended very high between two mountains. I had a picture taken wearing the traditional Atayal costume in front of a man-made waterfall.

When we went back to the city, we toured areas of interest including the tallest building in Taipei which had 101 floors. I chickened out. After a few days, we checked out of our hotel and took the high-speed train to Medy's residence in Taichung. The train travelled at 294–296 kilometres per hour.

Atayal costume - Wulai Taipei 1981

I recorded this fact in my small notebook because I was fascinated by the modern transport. I knew Japan had bullet trains, but I didn't expect Taiwan to have them. We reached Taichung in a few hours.

When Chen retired, he and Medy bought a modern two-bedroom apartment with an elevator to the fourth floor. It was in a good area near Ming Dao University. We were introduced to Yuen Yuen, an eight-year-old boy who was under Medy and Chen's care while his mother was at work. I struggled to talk to him in my rusty Mandarin. I practised my broken and choppy Mandarin on Chen and Yuen Yuen every day. It was awkward and sort of amusing, but we were able to get across our meaning while trying to understand each other. Agie did the same. Ate Beth couldn't speak Mandarin. We all translated her greetings and impressions for Chen and Yuen Yuen.

During our stay in Taichung, we looked around, did some shopping, and met some beautiful young Filipino workers at church on Sunday. Agie went back to the Philippines but Ate Beth and I stayed a few more days in Taichung.

It was wonderful to see Medy and Chen again. When we went to the airport to return to the Philippines, we took a modern, air-conditioned bus to Taipei International Airport. We had a pleasant view of the countryside along the highway, but it was a long trip. At the airport check-in, by chance, I met some old friends from my days working in Taipei. They gave me updates on mutual friends. What a small world!

When we returned to the Philippines, I joined my cousin Ate Beth on her trip to Iloilo, central Philippines. I hoped to go to my birthplace in . This was a time for memories. I had allotted time for this visit and I was ready. It was my first walk down this particular memory lane. Now was the time to do it. I wanted to visit the place I was born to find out whether it was the same as the place that appeared in my dreams. I had had a series of dreams about my birthplace. These dreams became frequent in the years before I went home. I could picture the narrow street going to our old big house in the farm that Tatay built and Madong Elementary School where the Masesar children were famous for our place on the honour roll every year. My eldest brother Tito, my elder sister Veronica, and I were on the honour roll. In my dreams, the road from the elementary school from which I graduated and the road going to our house always appeared. I also dreamed of my classmates. I had wanted to go back home for many years but I didn't have the means or opportunity while I was working and raising two children in a foreign country.

When we reached Iloilo City, Ate Beth and I stayed at my uncle's house. My father built this house when I was in my college years as I remember. My father had passed away in 2003 yet the house was standing strong. My aunt said that the roof of their neighbour's house, which was newer than theirs, had collapsed but the house that Tatay built stayed firm. I had seen my father's ingenuity and craftsmanship as a builder and carpenter. I felt proud that my father had built a solid house even if it was not ours, but my uncle's. Before his retirement, my uncle, an accountant, had been a manager at Shell.

I took pictures and videos of the house as a memento of my father's building skills. It had three bedrooms and an extension room for the housemaid. The water storage was made of solid cement from the roof of the house to the ground floor. It had a wire screen and a water tap at the bottom. The family used the water for daily use such as laundry, dishwashing, watering plants and cleaning. For drinking, they used bought bottled water.

Ate Beth and I scheduled a day to visit Madong, the place where I was born. She wanted to catch up with distant relatives in town. We took public transport there. I was amazed at my cousin's courage. She lived in the United States, but she takes public transport every time she visits her home in Iloilo. She was fluent in the native dialect (which I could also speak but with a noticeable accent) so she sounded like a local. She also had a lot of relatives in nearby towns and barrios. Ate Beth had a knack of discovering everyone's ancestry. Whenever she heard someone's surname she could trace her relationship to them, with diplomatic questions.

We had several jeepney transfers from one town to the other until we reached our destination. I was excited and at the same time apprehensive about what I might find. Would the farm and elementary school that held memories of my happiest childhood years still be there? I had dreamed of the place so it must have been beckoning for me to come back and visit.

When we arrived, we first went to Ate Beth's distant relative who had a house on a nearby farm. I later learned that the guy who met us knew my primary classmates Nonito and Bede.

When we walked towards Madong Elementary School, I was surprised to find that it looked exactly the same as during my primary grades, with only a few alterations. I took photos in delight as it hadn't been tampered with by any structural or environmental changes. It still looked provincial, like the old school I had known. I thanked the Lord that I was able to find the place as it was. I felt a connection and belonging right away. I was even more surprised when there were teachers waiting for me. They had been advised by the guy we first saw that I was coming. I had no recollection whatsoever of their names and who they were in my primary years. One of them was Mrs Partisala, who recognised me but unfortunately I couldn't remember her. She said she had been one of my primary school classmates and that she was retiring from teaching very soon. The school principal, Miss Biton, who unfortunately was not around to meet us, also knew about the Masesar family and our school achievements. The sister of my classmate Bede was also teaching there. I took some photos with some of the teachers who attended to us with the old school surroundings as background. I was given a tour of the old school. Nothing had changed much. There was an annex on the left side for home economics and more classrooms in the next building. I was so happy that the teachers were accommodating and very friendly to me although we didn't know each other.

After we said goodbye to the teachers at the Madong Elementary School, Ate Beth and I took a tricycle to Nonito's place. He was my primary school classmate and the valedictorian in our class. I was the salutatorian. I was lucky because he was out checking something in his front yard. Ate Beth knew him because she had been there the previous year when I asked her to find out about Nonito before my visit. I got off the tricycle, called to him and introduced myself. I didn't expect him to be so thin and frail, so different from the good-looking, smart boy I had known. I must have looked awful because I had a terrible attack of hay fever. I was sneezing and coughing and my eyes and nose were swollen. I must have looked like a cooked shrimp. The humidity didn't help. I was drenched with sweat and parched. What an impression for a first meeting with my primary school classmate after fifty-one years! When I asked about the small triangle of woods planted on the ground in the front yard he was inspecting, Nonito explained they were there to protect the roosters he was raising. Some of them were prized cockpit roosters. I told him we were going to visit our other classmate Petring who lived near our old house in Tuburan.

Nonito took this opportunity to make himself 'presentable'. He wasn't prepared for the surprise encounter or my unexpected arrival. When Ate Beth went to his place unexpectedly the previous year and introduced herself as my cousin, he had told her that of course he remembered me because I was his crush in primary school.

Ate Beth and I returned to the tricycle we had hired for the entire time we were there to visit one place after the other. The road to Tuburan was narrow, as in the olden days, but the big house of the Layadors was no longer there on the street corner. Instead, a bungalow had been erected. I took note of the way to our former house. It was like my dream. The rice fields were planted with rice, but the variety was very low, and the crops were almost touching the soil. It was not like the tall-stalked rice that my father used to plant. The road was muddy, so the tricycle had a hard time avoiding potholes.

When we reached Tuburan, I stopped at the creek when I heard the gush of water. I found the very spot where we used to take a short-cut down the stream when we were children. The mark of our old short-cut was still there. I didn't go down to peep as it was a bit bushy, but I made a video. I was glad to see the tall bamboos still standing, as if no years had passed by.

We reached Petring's house after several enquiries for directions from people in the neighbourhood. She lived in a small nipa hut with a balcony. I found it cute and welcoming. Her son was home but he said Petring was out near the banana plantation. After a few moments we saw his mother coming back. I recognised Petring straight away because of her squinted eye. She looked emaciated. Her hair was long and braided. Her son was good-looking. I was glad she had a son. She told me she was now a widow. Petring and I caught up on how life had been since we last parted during our primary grades over fifty years ago. Our former small house was occupied by my cousin on my mother's side. I knew about this because before I came to Iloilo, Nanay's relatives and Ben, my younger brother who had close contact with our mother's family, had told me that the former plantation was now owned by my cousin Nong Goding (Godofredo). Nong is a colloquial word to address an older male relative. I didn't bother going there because the exact place of my childhood house was now covered by banana trees and thick vegetations. It was sad.

It was so humid, and I was feeling uncomfortable in my silk-lined blouse, so I changed at Petring's house into the spare blouse I had brought. I felt comfortable with Petring. It was as if we were kindred spirits. I am always at ease with people who live in the countryside. They have a certain way of welcoming strangers. Although my roots were here in this place, they hadn't known or seen me since my childhood, yet I was welcomed as if I was one of them. After a long catch-up, Petring and I said our goodbyes.

Ate Beth and I went back to the main street, driven by the tricycle boy patiently waiting for us. We stopped occasionally at spots where I wanted to take pictures of my precious visit to the place I was born and the memories it evoked in me. I noticed that the tree at the corner of the street when I was young was still in the same spot. I couldn't comprehend how it could still be there. It was a small tree, not as big as the one I saw in my child's eye.

We went back to Nonito's place. This time, he had changed into a summer shirt and pants. He welcomed us in his house and invited us to be seated in the living room. He motioned to us the other room where there was an electric fan. The living room was hot and humid. He introduced us to his wife who was bedridden due to a bad fall. Nonito said that it would take thousands of pesos (around 85,000 almost AUD$2,125) for his wife to have surgery. They were waiting for funds from relatives overseas to help with the cost of the operation. Meanwhile, Nonito was looking after his wife. Sometimes his two sons relieved his round-the-clock care. He told me that Bede, our other honour roll classmate, was currently in Los Angeles and was sick with cirrhosis. Bede was planning to come home for good. He said our primary teacher, Mrs Domillo, was living in front of their house and was now at least 90 years old. I declined a visit because I was feeling really ill due to my non-stop sneezing. The unbearable heat didn't help. I was all swollen and puffy, but I agreed to have a picture taken with Nonito as a souvenir of my visit. I promised Nonito I would come back in two years' time so we could organise our elementary school reunion. It would not be until 2012 that I was able to go back.

Chapter 36

In 2008 my job was offshored during the bank's ongoing restructure. This second retrenchment didn't hit me as hard as the first. I was older and it was time for me to rethink my priorities. I was not yet of retirement age, so I couldn't afford to be without a job. All my life, almost a quarter of my earnings had gone to help the family and other charity donations. I managed to have holidays in other countries despite a tight budget and I was glad I did this before finances became tighter. There was no use looking for a job at the end of the year so I took advantage of the season to do things I couldn't do when I was working.

In January 2009, I looked for jobs again and after over 100 applications, I found some temporary work. I was struggling but I didn't touch my emergency funds. It was frustrating because there were three major share market crashes at that time, and my superannuation savings and small investments suffered significant losses. I didn't touch my superannuation, but my small investments made a loss. Despite this, I persevered in getting temporary jobs even if some of them treated me as if I were an imbecile with no brains.

I had always been a misfit at work, but I needed a constant flow of income, no matter how small, to live an independent life and not be dependent on handouts. Although I didn't pursue prestigious positions, I had been proud of my accomplishments. There was a time when I felt as if I shouldered the problems of the whole world alone. My strong faith helped me get through the most difficult times. Sometimes, it had been so hard that I was on the brink of life and death. This was especially true during and after the divorce. At that time, I lost my focus, I felt so rejected, unloved, as if everyone just wanted to take from me. When the crunch came, I was alone, bleeding, hurt, angry, deceived and neglected. These emotions created so much agony in my life that there were times I wanted to give up.

But I was proud and determined, so I picked up the pieces. Despite fear, anguish and deep pain, I persevered. I didn't let negative things ruin my life. I had to think of my children and my mother, father, brothers and sisters who were part of my life. I know most won't agree with me, but I believe God, the Blessed Mother Mary, and all the angels and saints helped me in times of trials. There were times when I didn't know what to do. There were times when I didn't want to pray anymore, but for some reason, I kept going back to church and praying. Even now, I never miss Sunday mass because this is my way of communicating with God.

Times had changed and so did I. I enrolled in the evening classes at Bankstown TAFE and took a Certificate III in Business Administration. I updated my computing and other skills so I could get jobs other than banking, which often restructured and shed employees. I was the oldest in the class, but I got on well with my classmates. Some of them were as young as eighteen years old. Maybe I was a misfit again, but I had fun because I love learning new things. It gave me joy and purpose in life and I was glad of my accomplishments as an older person when I got my certificate. My dearest friend, Sam took my graduation picture. My good friends, Mary Ann and Michael also attended my graduation. They were my moral support.

In January 2010, I went back to the Philippines for another visit and had a lovely time catching up with old friends and relatives. My friend from Bulacan, a few miles away from Manila, took me and several other friends to Baguio City, where we stayed for a week. We had a good time going around the tourist spots. I was disappointed to see that Baguio City, which was the pine tree city of the Philippines, was not as alluring as it used to be. The last time I had visited was during my college days. Now the mountainside was full of houses, not pine trees. On the way to the strawberry plantation, it was also full of squatter houses which ruined the view of the mountains.

When I came back, my cousin Ate Beth asked me to join her in their annual class reunion with her Nursing University classmates in Iloilo City. Their reunion last for several days with a lot of fun activities. Most of the classmates live in the United States and return to the Philippines every year to celebrate their reunion. I was honoured to have been invited to their gala night. It was interesting to watch them perform songs and dances on the stage. And to think that they were all over 70 years old! One could observe the real camaraderie between these classmates who had bonded through the years and knew how to enjoy themselves. They had picnics, outings, and school affairs. My cousin, Ate Beth, was good at making friends. She would have made a good diplomat.

I made an unexpected visit to barrio Tara-Tara when Ate Beth asked me to tag along with her. We were in a van with a group of nuns who were Ate Beth's classmates from St Paul's College, Iloilo. We were going to attend mass at a chapel erected in barrio Tara-Tara. Saint Therese Chapel was financed by one of Ate Beth's college classmates who lived in the United States. While we were waiting for the mass to start, I asked around if anybody knew Nang Judith and Nong Porping, my first cousins on Nanay's side. Nanay and her relatives came from Tara-Tara. I'd asked Nanay to give me a picture of Uncle Enrique, her youngest brother, before I left Sydney because I wanted to meet her side of the family. Nanay hadn't really been in touch with her family except her elder sister Natividad and the youngest, Uncle Enrique, the one we call Tay Adring. Our family gatherings were mostly with Tatay's big clan. We had lost contact with Nanay's relatives after we migrated to Quezon City, in the northern part of the Philippines. Nanay's family were poor so they hadn't travelled to visit us. I never met any of Nanay's relatives except Nanay's eldest sister's children who looked after us when we were young and were living in the farm.

One of the ladies I asked recognised me when I said my name, so she asked, 'Are you Nora, Leon's daughter who became Miss Stamp? I helped your dad collect stamps for you.' I wasn't expecting this. I couldn't believe that someone could remember me after such a long time. This lady was able to confirm this unknown fragment of my life story to me.

When I asked if they knew my cousins, Nang Judith and Nong Porping, they said yes. They pointed to the hilly side of the church where my cousins lived. I was so excited and surprised at the unexpectedness of it all. Mass had started so I couldn't go there. I secretly gave money to the boy beside me and asked him to call my cousins and let them know I was in church. In a small barrio, everybody knows everyone; news spreads quickly. After mass, I was even more surprised when Nang Judith, Nong Porping and the other first cousins came and embraced me. Nang Judith cried when she saw me. She was wearing black. She told me her husband had passed away. She was the one who had looked after me when I was growing up in the farm with my other siblings. Nong Porping was taller than most of the barrio people. He was well-off, having married well. In fact, his wife's relative owned the big house where we stayed for lunch after mass.

As our custom, I gave money to each of my relatives and the lady who recognised me. I was blessed to have met my mother's relations after all those long years. I believed then that God let me come to that place unplanned, for a special reason.

Never in my dreams had I ever expected to meet my relatives on Nanay's side. It had taken me a long time to find the courage to walk down that particular memory lane but when I did, I was blessed.

When my companions and I went back to the van to go back to Iloilo City, my relatives were there to wave goodbye to me and our group. It was sad as it was hello and goodbye. I don't know if I will meet them again. My only memory of them may be the picture I had taken of us before I left.

I had a few more days to spare before I went back to Sydney. I wanted to go back to Project 4, Quezon City where I spent my teenage and high school years. I wanted to see the old place and find out whether the people who lived there were still there. This was the place I lived until I got married and moved to Laguna where I bought our first house. I wanted to see how the place looked now. I had had updates from people leaving and migrating overseas, but I wanted to see it for myself. Perhaps it was time for me to really look back and revisit those old places without a trace of bitterness and sadness in my heart. I had carried these feelings all throughout the years in my struggles through life. Finally, I was ready to look back. I felt I had accomplished enough. I had been to the USA and Europe. It was time to come back to the place I grew up as a teenager and revisit the memories of my high school days which were part of what made me who I am.

My youngest brother Eddie drove me to Project 4, Quezon City. The roads we passed through were foreign to me. Nothing I had stored in my memory was familiar. There were so many changes – the roads, the streets, and the route going to Project 4 had become commercialised. I couldn't even see the old Stella Maris College, an exclusive girls' school in Cubao, Quezon City. We passed through the back route, I guess, because the Araneta Coliseum looked like a commercial place and not as distant to travel as when I was there. The road to Blue Ridge going to Quirino Hospital was built up with houses on both sides. It used to be barren and the hospital seemed to be very far away.

We found Aguinaldo Street where we used to live. It looked different. I was glad that some of the good neighbours still lived there. I was accompanied by my college best friend, Eden, who knew Malou, my younger sister's best friend. We went to visit Malou's house first. Malou said that my former neighbour Dulce still lived in the same house. We knocked at the house, but her brother answered. Dulce had bought the house that used to be their aunt's, so we went there. I had luck on my side because Dulce and her husband were there. She is married with children. She still looked pretty and hadn't changed much. The house had a top floor now. Most of the houses before were uniformly built as public housing houses which were ultimately sold as private residences to the occupants. Dulce and I caught up on our life's events from the time I left. I didn't know she had graduated from the same high school as me. I couldn't believe it when she told me. I thought she graduated from the affluent girls' school, Stella Maris College. She said, 'Are you kidding? We couldn't afford that school.' During our conversation, I learned that she attended our high school class reunions regularly. She invited me to join in, but I hesitated, saying I didn't know my classmates anymore. She said not to worry. I could come casually and join the fun. I didn't take up the offer as I was going back to Sydney. Dulce accepted me as her friend on Facebook and that was the start of my continuing liaison with her. Little did I know that it was the beginning of a joyful communication with most of my high school classmates all over the world, before I actually met them in the Philippines during our 50th High School reunion in 2014. I went back just for that event. It was well worth it! It was a very happy reunion. I met classmates, some of whom I wouldn't have recognised were it not for their familiar-sounding names. My high school best friend Ching, who lived in Canada, also came for the occasion.

When I came back to Sydney, I was in and out of temporary jobs, but I felt lucky to earn even a small amount of income. Finally, I found an agent who took me on as an older client and got me a one-year contract at an insurance company. My young tutor bullied me. When I made a slight mistake and didn't conform to her way of thinking or use her specific wordings, she lambasted and embarrassed me with a dressing down within earshot of other staff. I took all of this in silence as I was on contract, but on the third month, I blew my top and marched off to human resources. We resolved the issue in front of my immediate chief and our team leader. My other workmate, who was more senior than the bully, guided me through the processes when I had questions. I had a pleasant working relationship with her and the rest of the staff until I finished my contract. Everyone else was pleasant.

During this time, a young workmate in our department passed away. It was a shock because she was full of life. She had an awful cough at the office one Friday before the weekend. We learned that she passed away on the weekend when she did not come to work the following Monday.

While we all grieved, a greater grief overtook me because my beloved friend Sam passed away the following month. It devastated me because he was the only person who understood me. We understood each other despite all of our human failings. We were both givers, so we had this affinity. He was a loner despite being likeable and thoughtful to his friends.

I made arrangements for his funeral, liaised with his brother, his only kin in England, and when his brother arrived, the funeral service was attended by my friends and relatives. None of his friends came despite my sending several invitations. His death left a void.

When I finished my contract with the insurance company, I wanted to get away from all the grief. I decided to take a long break overseas.

Chapter 37

Two important events took place during these travels. First, I reconciled with my children after a long time living separate lives. Second, was the sad discovery of the death of my two best friends from primary school.

My children and I decided to have a family holiday in the Philippines and do some island-hopping. The Philippines has 7,200 islands so we planned and booked destinations we wanted to explore. This was the first time that we were able to go on a real holiday as a family during my children's adult years.

I asked my cousin Pinky if we could have a big reunion again at their place like the previous ones I had attended. It was always fun when she organised it because she attended to the minutest details. It was a good feeling being surrounded by relatives coming from other countries and from other parts of the Philippines. My children had never experienced our big family reunions. When I say big, the number would be up to 200 including first, second, third, fourth and even fifth generations of our parents' families. We, the close first cousins, belong to the second generation. My children were excited when I told them about this family reunion. It would be their first experience like this and they would meet relatives for the first time. We flew to the Philippines after spending Christmas with Nanay in the nursing home, part of our family tradition. My children enjoyed the reunion and met cousins, uncles and aunts for the first time. It was a very happy occasion. The welcoming of the New Year was full of fun. We had our own firecrackers and as before, because Pinky's family lived in an affluent suburb, the firecrackers all over the place were almost as impressive as in Sydney.

We stayed at their place overnight then flew on New Year's Day to Palawan Island on the start of our island-hopping holiday. We went to exotic El Nido at the northern tip of Palawan. This is a beautifully secluded island where one can feel close to nature because of its unspoilt beauty. My son booked a boat trip package for an adventure trip. He hired a private boat – only us, the boatman and the oarsman. They were very skilled but it still scared me when we passed through the intersection of the open China sea and the Philippine sea. The water looked blackish and the waves lashed at our boat, rocking it through the crests and troughs. I thought it would capsize with the size of the waves that flapped relentlessly on our tiny boat. I was alarmed but I didn't show my panic and prayed hard. This holiday was a means of bringing the family closer together and I knew that this was a test of my faith in the Lord. The scary, rough journey ended when we turned left to the entrance of one of the mountain caves.

Everything seemed to go wrong. When we reached our destination, we couldn't get off on a hidden beach between the high rocks. The beach wasn't visible at high tide. Some people from other boats had braved the passage, but it looked so deep that it would be too risky. Other travellers didn't bother to get off their boats. Our boatman turned back and stopped at the next beach in an enclosed cove. It was a safe enclosure, which was a pleasant surprise.

The boatman and his assistant prepared a special native dish for us. They barbecued pork and fish in the inner sanctum of the cave. We ate lunch and enjoyed the serenity and beauty of the enclosed cove. Other families who came ahead of us had already settled on the other side of the beach and were eating their lunch. We waved to them. Later, another tourist boat arrived, and the passengers joined us on the beach. The boatman told us that this was the place where fishermen sheltered when the seas were rough, and they couldn't go home. Sometimes they stayed there for a few days until the seas were calm.

On our way back, the boatman took the other route which he said was the safer way. He said he was about to go this way before but because he didn't see panic in my face, he continued on. My goodness! If only he knew how my heart had somersaulted in fright, worried that we might be engulfed by the huge waves. I was afraid that despite our life jackets, my children and I would drown in the rough sea on a supposedly happy family holiday. We continued, stopping at other beautiful beaches on different small islands. The water on the inlet shores was calmer, as if untouched by the turbulent sea at the meeting between the Pacific Ocean and the China Sea.

We went back to Palawan City the next day, another six-hour drive on a long, winding road. We booked another boat trip on the Underground River at Puerto Princesa. This time we wore life jackets and sat in pairs in a narrow boat. We had a hilarious boat guide who joked all the way. This assuaged our fears at the darkness, the restricted space between the walls, and the depth of the river. At the end of the cave was the cathedral-like ceiling of the underground river.

From Palawan, we went back to Manila and from there we flew to Bohol, another island in central Philippines. We took a day trip to Lombok and booked a beautiful cruise along the Lombok River. We had native food and were serenaded by the locals. The younger children were so skilful performing the native dances, which were a joy to behold. We then went to Chocolate Hills, considered one of the wonders of the world. Our local guide during my first visit to the island told me they were named by an American dignitary who toured the area because the tiny mounds resembled Hershey's Kisses. We stayed for a few days in Bohol before we went to Cebu City via a rivercat ferry. We weren't able to tour Cebu because it was the feast of Santo Nino, the Patron Saint of Cebu. The streets were crowded with people and the traffic was terribly jammed. The locals celebrated the festival with much flourish. Our time was limited because we booked for our next journey the following day to Iloilo City, another island of the Philippines in the Visayan Region.

In Iloilo, we stayed at a friend's place in Pototan, a suburb of Iloilo City. My uncle and aunt lived in Iloilo City, so we visited them before continuing our journey. The taxi service we hired for the day was owned by my aunt's cousin. We felt safe going around. I knew Sam, the driver from my first visit to Iloilo City. He looked after me as a relative and my children liked him instantly. The next day we packed our bags for our new destination, Boracay Island. We were surprised when Sam and his co-driver offered to drive us there. He said it would be quicker and safer than catching a public bus with our luggage. I was even surprised when he took us to the place where I was born, knowing that it has a special place in my heart.

We passed by Madong Elementary School. I was sad because the principal who knew me and the teacher, Mrs Partisala, whom I had chatted with four years before, had retired. I was also sad to learn that Nonito and Bede, my primary school buddies, had passed away. I had promised Nonito I would come back for our primary class reunion but I wasn't able to come back that year. I guess it wasn't meant to be. The new principal of the Madong Elementary School was Hector, a young gentleman who attended to us and introduced me to his new staff. They were all pleasant and we had our pictures taken. I was glad I could still connect with my former school despite the absence of the people from my generation.

From Madong, Sam drove us through scenic places with water views; we visited old churches and passed through the mountains on our way to my aunt's place in Antique. Auntie Connie, my father's youngest sister, lived in this part of Panay Island. We had lunch at her place before we continued our journey to Boracay Island, a famous tourist attraction at the tip of Panay Island, near Antique province.

When we reached the wharf to take our ferry to Boracay Island, Sam and his co-driver had to drive back to Iloilo City, a six-hour drive. I was glad he had given us a private tour instead of letting us ride the public bus with our luggage. He charged me a reasonable fare for the journey. He was really kin because he saved us from the trouble of dragging our luggage to board a bus. We had had a comfortable and pleasant journey while he entertained us, telling us stories about the places we passed by, to the delight of my children. I love this about our culture – concern and affection that money can't buy. I gave Sam good compensation for his goodwill. I would have given him more if I could have.

Davis booked us at a resort near the mountains on Boracay Island, not in the main tourist area. It was a secluded place with its own private beach. We had to take a tricycle to go to the main tourist area. It was there when I got sick with diarrhoea and was placed on a drip with the doctor and nurse visiting me every four hours.

Two days later we flew back to Manila from Kalibo, Aklan, then home to Australia. Daina went back ahead due to work commitments and Davis returned to his place in Cairns, where he was working, via Darwin International Airport.

Chapter 38

In February 2012, I decided to embrace a new course in life. I had no job to go back to, so I decided to retire, using my savings. I had had enough of looking for employment at my age and doing temporary part-time jobs. It was hard to compete with younger people's more advanced skills. I consolidated my superannuation funds which had diminished due to the several share market's crashes from the 1990s onwards and lived on a tighter budget. I was good at budgeting because despite my meagre income, I could always save. I had been working since I was young, and I felt now was the time to relax and leave the hurried pace of life behind.

I applied for membership at Sing Australia and I also became a member at the NSW Writer's Centre as well as doing volunteer work with St Vincent de Paul Society. My activities with these groups gave me an incentive to interact with others. I found new friends and learned new things. I had extra expenses despite my concessions, but I was glad I had retired.

I also enrolled in zumba classes. I enjoyed this healthy lifestyle and interaction with other people and my teachers were fun to work out with. I also walk to complement my exercises. I do simple calisthenics if I fail to do my walk. These activities give me a sense of belonging and purpose in life.

Our Ashbury Sing Australia group rehearsals are held every Monday evenings. I love the camaraderie. Villy, our young conductress, has a beautiful soprano voice. We, the members, are of mature age, but she enjoys what she does, and it is always a joy to rehearse with her. She shares her stories of training in the army and guides us through difficult new songs and sighs with a long 'Ah.......' and a wide smile of satisfaction after the end of a well-rendered favourite song, especially a love song. She is a romantic at heart. Our pianist Heather is a quiet one who expresses her love of music through her piano. Our group leaders are fantastic.

Sing Australia, a national group based in Melbourne, was founded by Colin Slater, our director. In New South Wales, there were seven groups when I joined – Gordon, Narrabeen, Collaroy, Wollongong, Sutherland, Penrith and Ashbury, my group. Later on, more groups were formed all over Australia and in NSW there are new groups in St George and Kiama. Our group performs at nursing homes and retirement villages. Sometimes we attend public gigs upon invitation. On occasions like this, we wear our teal uniform with a beautiful waratah flowered scarf with a black skirt or pants. We join other groups and perform as Sing Australia. One of our public gigs was held in the Town Hall on Reserve Forces Day in 2012. It was a memorable experience for me. I was happy to receive a certificate personally signed by the then Governor-General, Quentin Bryce. We also have national gatherings in different states. Sing Australia also has overseas tours for those who can afford it.

These activities ease my loneliness and lighten any problems with family, health and the shocking news from the world we live in. It took me a long time to relax and get accustomed to a slower pace, but ultimately, I learned to enjoy having more time. I think this is just the beginning of a better life. As I grow older, I see a lot of opportunities. Now that my children are older and have lives of their own, I am free to explore my interests. I don't owe anything to anyone and I don't feel guilty if I allow myself the indulgence to be free, happy and enjoy the fruits of my labour.

It has taken me a long, long time to look back without tears in my eyes. I only started walking down memory lane when I went back to my birthplace in 2008. Now, when I look back, I have no regrets because I did my best despite the sorrows and tears, despite the loneliness and fear, despite the hurtful words hurled at me. Despite the difficulties, I survived. I am proud to have done it all, and all in my own way!

This has been my journey. It was a lonely journey because most of the time, I walked alone. If I bled along the way, if I suffered in silence, it was because this was my way. It is true that time heals. I was able to leave behind my unhappy past. Maturity comes with age, and although my thinking was mature even when I was young, my experiences made me learn to accept the things that I cannot change, as they say.

I was always guided by my faith which was handed down to me by generations of strong-willed and determined ancestors. I acquired courage from my father and tenderness, love and wisdom from my mother. Without my strong faith and the love of my parents, I don't know where I would be. For this, I thank them with all my heart. My father is now resting in peace, and my mother has passed away. I know I haven't failed them. I owe them a lot for their guidance and the values they instilled in me.

I don't know what lies ahead. I have learned to live each day of my life – to appreciate the rising of the sun, the many things I can do with my spare time, and to indulge in my hobbies and interests. We, the so-called baby boomers, have contributed to society and our generation did a great deal of good before the advent of modern technology. We expect the younger generation to value the morals and the good teachings of the past, in spite of the influence of too much sex, drugs and violence in the media, movies and television. Life is still beautiful despite the odds.

Australia has given me and my children the freedom to make choices and to make use of opportunities. We have given our all, as much as we have taken. We appreciate the beauty of this wide brown land, its people, arts, culture, beaches, educational opportunities and the rail system that allowed us to travel interstate. I love Sydney, Canberra, Queensland, Cairns, Melbourne, Tasmania and the rest of Australia that I have yet to explore. It is a sunburnt country, but I love it just the same. I have travelled overseas many times but coming back home to Australia brings me the greatest pleasure.

Chapter 39

Each of us is given a journey. No one can walk the journey for us. It is a unique path. I had a lonely journey. I had to create my own path for survival. I focused on what I wanted to achieve in a certain time frame. At the back of my mind were the loved ones who were part of the plan. I couldn't afford to be complacent.

I met a lot of people on my journey and I believe that you meet a person for a reason. Perhaps it's part of growing up, of knowing pain, hardship, joy and compassion that taught me to accept the inevitable. In our respective journeys, we cannot prevent ourselves from getting hurt, yet we must get up again and face life's harsh realities. After all, life is what we make it and despite the thorns and sorrows in our journey, there are also moments of happiness, joy, love and forgiveness. It is up to us to see and appreciate the many blessings that were given to us even in subtle ways which we sometimes fail to notice because we are so busy and distracted. There is also wisdom in the Biblical quotation of Ecclesiastes 3:1–4 about time.

>   [1]There is an appointed time for everything, and a time for every affair under the heavens.
>   [2]A time to be born, and a time to die; a time to plant, and a time to uproot the plant.
>   [3]A time to kill, and a time to heal; a time to tear down, and a time to build.
>   [4]A time to weep, and a time to laugh; a time to mourn, and a time to dance.

I have no regrets for what I have done and for the life I have chosen. If I made mistakes, those mistakes made me strong and helped me become a better person. I have learned hard, and despite the difficulties, I have always carried on the wisdom my parents handed down, especially my mother. Their words of wisdom were passed on from the previous generation to the next. I appreciate the values my parents inculcated in me because they guided me not to take the easy road, but to take the road that was chosen for me. I had a difficult journey, but I am proud to have triumphed against most of the odds. Had I let the hurtful words, the insults, the bullies, the people who tried to drag me down to utmost despair overtake my purpose in life, I wouldn't be where I am now.

I could have wallowed in self-pity. Some people are cruel. They wreck your self-confidence, your self-esteem, and your determination to do better. I was lucky to have listened to my parents' wisdom, to have stayed close to the few friends who were there for me through the good and the bad times, the real friends who have been with me through all the years of my life. I may not have had a happy marriage, but I had a very close-knit family, relatives and friends who were my anchor throughout my struggles in life. My children carry on the legacy of the wisdom of my generation, and for this, I am thankful.

I spent most of my working career in the banking industry in Australia. In my high school and college days I did not excel in mathematics, algebra, geometry or physics. I took a job that was daunting because I had no choice. I was amazed when my brain was able to absorb abstract concepts. I focused my mind on succeeding because I had a family to feed. I built my career in the industry and it was my bread and butter for years. I stayed in my job knowing I was assured of a constant flow of income. It was a stable income and no matter how difficult it was for me to adjust and how small the income was, it was better than aiming for an ideal job which had no sure income. I couldn't afford to deprive my family of a decent life, nor those relatives who depended on me for support.

I might have chosen the wrong career or made a wrong decision, but I couldn't afford a gap in my income. If I had looked for other jobs and lacked a constant flow of income, it could have been fatal. I was determined to give my children a good education and a stable life and help relatives in need of financial assistance. To achieve this, I had to set aside my lofty dreams. It is amazing how the brain can work given no choice but to analyse, study, adapt and learn, in order to survive. I didn't know I could handle figures, balance funds, deal with spreadsheets and accounts, and manage millions of payments. Who would have thought that a literary-leaning person like me would end up in such a job? I am proud that I had built my career in different aspects of banking although it was not my line of interest. Had I been a journalist exposed to a lot of dangers, where would I be now? Would I have a family of my own, or still be wandering around, or be six feet below the ground? There are injustices all over the world. Would I be able to suppress the truth and not speak my mind on what I thought was not right?

Looking back, after all the hardships and obstacles in my life – the snide remarks about my small stature; condescending attitudes of those who were well-off; being hungry and deprived of even basic necessities; and being poor in general – have pushed me to achieve more and to prove that no matter how difficult the job or situation was, I could always make it. My mind had the capacity to adjust to any challenge, to grasp the seemingly abstract and difficult concepts. I think these circumstances shaped me into what I am. My children and I have been through a lot, but we have maintained the legacy of love, family bonding and togetherness which are essential. Others may not agree, but this is my life, my own story, and I cannot have it any other way.

In our life journey, we meet different kinds of people. Some people hurt us and some we fall in love with. We are lucky if we find true love and live happily ever after. For a couple to live a long life together, they have to go hand-in-hand through their journey. It doesn't work when only one partner does the walking and the other does the dragging. 'It takes two to tango.'

Our path in life can sometimes be visible and easy to tread but most of the time there is no path. We have to take the risk of finding our own way. Will it be to freedom? To more risk? Have we chosen the wrong path? The important thing is to try to find the right path until we reach our desired destination.

I chose my own path, or…. was I destined to walk a road with no path? Sometimes we have a long and difficult journey in life because there are a lot of thorns along the way, and to continue on is a very lonely road! Each one of us has our own rivers to cross, and I guess it is how we manage to cross turbulent waters that makes us the way we are. For me, life is a learning process. I have learned from my mistakes. I think it is true that things happen for a reason. Each of us lives differently, and it is up to us to make a difference, whether to improve our lives, or to let things happen as they should. Some people make it, some don't. Mine was a difficult journey but I found it colourful and full of surprises, which made it worthwhile. I have soared through it all, and I'm happy to be free. Now I look back without tears in my eyes. I have accepted what life had given me.

I continue to communicate with old friends and acquire new ones. Through Facebook, I have up-to-date communication with my high school friends. I developed new friendships through my activities with Sing Australia, my volunteer work with St Vincent de Paul, my membership of Writing NSW (previous NSW Writers' Centre), and with my Writer's Group. Life is beautiful despite its twists and turns. When my mother passed away on 7 October 2014, my life took a new direction – but that is another story. This is where I leave off for the next chapter of my life.

Glossary

adobo	way of cooking pork, fish or chicken
ale, aling	a respectful term to address an older woman (aling is used before the given name)
amargoso	Spanish name of bitter gourd
ampalaya	Tagalog name of bitter gourd
andador	child's walking frame
arapunaya	a purplish leaf with green streaks which probably belongs to the aloe vera family
ate	elder sister
balimbing	a fruit which tasted sweet-sour and looks like a star when cut horizontally
banana cue	bananas cooked in oil and brown sugar
banga	clay pot
bangus	milk fish
barkada	mate
barrio	neighbourhood or village (Spanish)
Bayanihan	traditional Filipino system of mutual help
bayong	tall, matted bag made of dried nipa leaves
bibingka	snack made of whole glutinous rice cooked in a clay pot

Glossary

bilo-bilo	small glutinous rice balls
bilong-bilong	type of fish
bolo	scythe
buko	soft flesh of young green coconut
calamansi	Filipino lime
camachiles	a bland fruit ranging from green or yellow to purple when ripe
carabao	water buffalo
cavan	Spanish unit for measuring rice
champorado	breakfast dish of glutinous rice mixed with dark cocoa and brown sugar
chato	a children's game with sticks
chicos	a brown round sweet fruit (also known as sapodilla)
cogon	type of grass
gabi	taro
galunggong	type of fish
ginamos	shrimp paste
guinatan halo-halo	a mixture of sweet potatoes, ripe native banana, purple taro, tapioca, and ripe shredded jackfruit flesh
guinatan	any food cooked with coconut cream
gulaman	gelatine
halo-halo	mixed iced drink
Hiligaynon	magazine published in the Ilongo dialect
hito	type of fish like an eel
Iglesia ni Kristo	Church of Christ
Ilocos Norte	northern Philippines
Ilongo	dialect
jeepney	twin-bench small bus used for transport
kamote	sweet potato

Glossary

kaymito	green or purple round fruit with a soft white flesh
Kinaray-a	dialect
kuhol	escargot
kumare	godmother
kumpare	godfather
kumusta ka?	How are you?
kuya	elder brother
labatiba	big water bag
linas	separating rice grains with feet
Liwayway	literary magazine published in Tagalog
makahiya	weed meaning touch-me-not
malunggay	vegetable shaped like a four-leaf clover
Mamang	mother-in-law
mano po	touching the forehead with the back of an elder's hand in a sign of respect
mare	term used to address a godmother
mareng	female Godmother of child
merienda	teatime
moringa	a leaf vegetable
nanay	mother
nang	abbreviation of Manang, a term to address elder female relative
nipa hut	traditional Filipino house made from nipa leaves and bamboo poles
nipa	mats
nong	term of address for an older male relative
nonoy	pet name for cousin
palitaw	snack made of ground glutinous rice
pamanhikan	a man and his family asking for the hand of a woman (literally climbing the stairs)
pancit molo	Iloilo soup

Glossary

pangos	chewing sugar cane
pansit	Filipino noodles
pantat	Visayan name for type of fish like eel
parol	star decorations
pasalubongs	treats
patay-gutom	riff-raff, literally starved-to-death people
patis	fish sauce
pato	thin flat stone used in the game piko
piko	children's game with a stone and markings on the ground also known as skip, hop and step
pinipig	soft green rice
pochero	pork stew mixed with cooking bananas and bok choy leaves
pulutan	savoury snacks, the Filipino equivalent of tapas
puto	snack made of ground glutinous rice
saba	variety of banana
sabong	cockfighting
salakot	triangular hat made of bamboo slats
saluyot	native green leafy vegetable
santilmo	dialect word for ghost
santol	cottonfruit tree with round yellow fruit with a white juicy flesh and brown seeds
sapin-sapin	rice cake
sapodilla	brown round sweet fruit (also known as chicos)
sapsap	type of fish
sari-sari	convenience store
seneguelas	small round fruit, greenish-purple when ripe
sipa	children's game
suman	glutinous rice cake

Glossary

suso	spiral snail
tabi-tabi	excuse me
tanglad	lemon grass
tapa	beef
tatay	father
tay	uncle
tilapia	type of fish
tinola	soup made with chicken, moringa and ginger
tio	uncle, respectful term for older man
tosperina	whooping cough
tuba	fermented coconut wine
tuyo	salted dried herring
ube	purple taro
ubod	core of the coconut palm

Acknowledgements

This book was a product of a recurring dream about my birthplace.

Thank you my dearest cousin Beth Harper, for taking me to my birthplace and encouraging me to share my story; cousins Cynthia Abano and family, Manuel and Connie Rose de Lima for making my homecomings happy, Saturnino Borra who helped me fill the gaps in my family history, and Caroline and Gunnar Lien for taking us around Norway.

Thanks to my family who were always there for me and the loving memory of those who have gone.

Thanks to my dear friends Ching Blas Muego, Eden Sanglay, Anita Tadeo, Milagros Tetangco, Gilda Balasoto, George and Emily Villaroman, Teresita and Danny de Leon, Angelita Berlanga, Gerhard and Des Mueller, Catherine Piraino, Cindy Rosenmeir, Alan Popplewell and Elena Calingasan, for going out of your way to make a difference.

Thank you Madong Elementary School for the beautiful memories, my Quirino High School batchmates for the happy reunions. Thanks to Sing Australia and my Ashbury Group for our camaraderie, gigs, the well-being that comes from singing, and all the people I have met along the way – those who made me cry, and those who made me happy.

A big thank you to my non-fiction writer's group at the Writing NSW convened by Suzanne Little. Through your support, honest feedback and interest in the chapters I shared, I gained confidence to tell my story.

Thanks to Laurel Cohn and Associates for your manuscript development guidance and a big thank you to my wonderful copy editor Pamela Hewitt.

Thanks to Ashley Kalagian Blunt of the Writing NSW (formerly NSW Writer's Centre) and Joel Naoum who helped me publish this book.

And most of all, thank you my children for making my life meaningful.

www.ingramcontent.com/pod-product-compliance
Lightning Source LLC
Chambersburg PA
CBHW021141080526
44588CB00008B/154